D0982654

Above the Fall Line

For Leslie,
with my best
wishes.
Happiest of lives
to you —

Above the Fall Line

The Trail from White Pine Cabin

Amy Blackmarr

A Blackman

MERCER UNIVERSITY PRESS • MACON • 2003

ISBN 0-86554-901-X
MUP/H664

2003 Mercer University Press
6316 Peake Road
Macon, Georgia 31210-3960

First Edition.

Book design by Mary-Frances Burt

∞The paper used in this publication meets the minimum requirements
of American National Standard for Information Sciences—Permanence
of Paper for Printed Library Materials, ANSI Z39.48-1992.

Library of Congress Cataloging-in-Publication Data

Blackmarr, Amy.
 Above the fall line : the trail from White Pine Cabin / Amy
Blackmarr.—1st ed.
  p. cm.
 ISBN 0-86554-901-X (hardcover : alk. paper)
 1. Blackmarr, Amy. 2. Dahlonega Region (Ga.)—Biography. 3.
Country life—Georgia—Dahlonega Region. 4. Mountain life
—Georgia—Dahlonega Region. 5. Dahlonega Region (Ga.)—
Social life and customs. 6. Natural history—Georgia—
Dahlonega Region. I. Title.
 F294.D13B56 2003
 975.8'273—dc21
                                              2003010592

Grateful acknowledgment is made to Weatherhill, Inc. for permission to use the
excerpt by Sen Rikyu from *Tea Life, Tea Mind* by Soshitsu Sen XV.

The essay contained in "Rewriting Ulysses," entitled "Ulysses Sails Into Port," first
appeared in the Spring 1999 issue of *Oxford American: A Journal of Good Southern
Writing.*

The essay "Hot Chow Chow" was previously broadcast on Georgia Public Radio's
Georgia Gazette.

To Joe Stofiel

What will happen can't be stopped: aim for grace.

ANN BEATTIE
"Learning to Fall"

Warm and affectionate thanks to Robbie Niles and Catherine Emory; Aunt Helen, Uncle Johnny, and my Outler cousins (especially John); Teresa Wright; Aunt Rose and Uncle Burns; Pat Kleinhans and Sue Mattison; Dr. Lisa Johnson; Claudia Gibson; Lyn Hopper; Tony Burnham; Rev. Marti Keller; Deborah G. and John Ed Smith; Dr. Michael L. Johnson; Dr. Elizabeth Schulz; Dr. Gerald Masinton; Dr. Joshua McKinney; Mark Warren; Lindy Harrell; Jenn Green; Lou Ann Thomas; Kevin Manus; Dad; Mom; and Kelly and Christopher—for the countless ways in which I depended on them all throughout the writing of this book.

contents

*...an untrodden wilderness, stretching through
many a Carolina and Mexico of the soul.*

THOREAU, The Journals

wild places

It was a winter day, cold and sunny and fragrant with
wet leaves, when I came to live in Uncle Johnny's Blue
Ridge Mountain cabin. I did not plan to stay. In two years,
I'd decided, I'd be living in a cottage on the Gulf Coast of
Florida, with the sound of the sea outside my breakfast-
room window. I'd feed my leftover toast to the gulls and
dig coquinas at ebb tide and furnish my den with soft sofas
in pale shades of light.

But the raw-boned earnestness of this mountain
country, its honest and uncritical affection, took me by
surprise. Like an awakened lover, it wrapped its arms
around me and refused to let me go, coaxed me to taste and
breathe in again, touch and hold, hear and live. Hiking
down the hill to the spring U.J. had told me about, I
stepped over a fallen pine, and its fragrance brought me up
short, as though I'd remembered something I had forgotten.

Farther down I was astonished to find I could smell the spring before I reached it. I could even taste the water in the air.

And I could *see* again, too. I found clumps of coral mushrooms, pockets of moss, leaves with their colors still vibrant from autumn: violet, scarlet, yellow. Wild holly. Blue berries in the ground cover. Pinecones, long and smooth and slender, or round and fat and sharp to touch.

Before I came to North Georgia, I was living in a hand-built hippie house of steps in northeastern Kansas. From the tower room, where I slept, to the bathroom and back were fifty-two steps, small and narrow, of uneven proportions. The house was sloppily built and the bottom floor was brick and the walls were uninsulated limestone. As I sat reading in the evenings, drafts from the windows teased the loose hair at my temples, and my hands were always cold.

I didn't like the House of Steps. It felt inhospitable from the start. I rented it because my dogs and I needed a place in the country where we could run, and it wasn't far from the University of Kansas in Lawrence, where I had entered graduate school. I did manage to make a home of the place eventually, but it was a chillier sort of home than I liked, and the four agonizing years it stood for ironed some new wrinkles into the rough cloth of my understanding about who I thought I was and what I thought I knew. When my time there was up, I fled back home to Georgia like a refugee.

I'm a native flatlander, from Irwin County in South Georgia, where peanuts and cotton thrive in sandy, fossil-laden soil left bleached by ancient oceans, where brown ponds alive with turtles and large-mouth bass lie calm and warm under water oaks and pines. It is a mild, unchanging, quiet land, a soft chair on a screened porch when the wisteria's in bloom.

From up here in North Georgia I can see farther, and the world shifts and reorganizes itself in all these different lights that stretch like lazy cats across the blue hills. If in summer the ridge is a hazy blur under clouds, in winter I can make out individual trees and the old fire tower on Black Mountain. I can even, on the clearest days, make out the Appalachian Trail, that thin ribbon of dirt that weaves together all these eastern geographies and then moves on and on, past the place where my vision can no longer follow. Up here my vision expands with the light and the mountains fill it. The mountains are my frontier and my horizon.

Seasons are passionate here above the fall line. Winter is stubborn. Ice has bound me in for days. The threat of tornadoes I would have chuckled at in Kansas has driven me into the storage room with my dogs. The brittle pines and tender young hemlocks bear down and finally snap under the weight of wind and ice and snow, and the woods become a child's neglected playroom, her toys tossed aside and broken.

A professor of mine used to quote a writer who lamented how all the new poetry was about Loss. Write something else, said my professor. Leave out those lost babies, lost lovers, dead pets. Find something new. I used to worry that Loss was going to sneak into my essays and I wouldn't be able to write it out before they got published.

But this book is a little about Loss—of identity, confidence, boyfriend and best dog and pride. Because it turns out that sometimes, no matter how you try to remind it of all you've achieved, Loss just insists on hanging out at the center of your life for a while. It ushers you around by the elbow, shows you some startling truths about yourself, knocks you on your back and puts its size-sixteen boot on your chest. Then one day it stares you in the face and you're shocked by how much it's begun to look like you.

And like a winter blast of mountain air, that recognition cuts clean through to your bones. It's like a cold rag on your face after a long sleep, and you can't help it: you wake up. You refuse to die into your failure. You stop letting the small deaths convince you that you've suffered a bigger one. You make some coffee and move on.

You go outside and walk around with your dogs, cut a sprig of laurel for your blue vase, crush sassafras leaves in your palm and hold them up to your face. You strike out into the woods and find a trail. You watch for deer and woodpeckers, black snakes and bears. You name the wildflowers. You name the trees. Then one day, that great heartbreak you've been nursing suddenly gives way and no longer shields you from the heartbreak of your joy. And you can hardly believe it, how you've fallen in love with the whole laughing, welcoming world—which has always, you realize, always been in love with you.

White Pine Cabin
February 21, 2002

Above the Fall Line

The Trail from White Pine Cabin

trail head: White Pine Cabin

Uncle Johnny has come to install me. We're standing at opposite ends of the futon in White Pine Cabin, where I've come with my dogs to hide out for a while.

The place is U.J.'s family retreat, but he's offered it to me as a recovery room from the trauma of graduate school and some other things I've been brooding over. It's really no big deal. I don't have pancreatic cancer. I haven't lost a leg. But I've been ditched by my boyfriend, my therapist, and my identity and I'm feeling wobbly.

U.J. and I are making space for Grandmama's old card table, which will serve as my computer desk. He grabs the futon. "You get that end," he says in a tone that leaves no room for argument.

I bristle. Like my little gray dog Max, who will dig out from under a fence if he has to go to China first, I resent any challenge to my self-direction.

But this day I hold my tongue. U.J. is not a person I argue with except when my ego is large and imposing—which it is (at the moment) *not*. I sigh and move my end of the futon.

"That's the dedicated line for your computer," U.J. says, nodding toward a socket cover. I thank him, but it hardly seems enough. He and Aunt Helen have put in a phone line, a bigger refrigerator, a new front door with a window, and made a score of other improvements since I told them I was coming. Generosity so large can be overwhelming when you've nothing to return but your company.

Now U.J. is instructing me in the most efficient way to set the thermostat for the heat pump. "Don't turn it up all at once," he tells me, pointing to the red light that warns me when the electric coils come on. He shoots me a wry grin. "The power company really likes it when you do that."

This wee cabin is a single room plus a half-loft for sleeping, although the screened porch doubles the living space most of the year, and the front porch is wide enough for rocking chairs, if I had a mind to put some there. All unfinished white pine, the cabin was intended as a well-house for a home that got built in a neighboring county instead.

My "den" is thirteen feet by sixteen, big enough for the futon, two small bookcases, and the card table. My "kitchen" is here, too—a short counter, some shelves, the refrigerator, and a utility sink. A toaster oven and hot plate allow for a little cooking; a tiny microwave warms the leftovers. In the corner behind the bathroom door, a wooden bar holds my old turquoise silk Christmas dress and a canvas blazer. I've crammed books into every available niche.

Outside, my cousins' childhood wagon, brown with rust, sits in the pine straw near steps that lead down from the front porch to a lower-level storage room and shed. Steps by the side porch lead down to an enclosed outdoor shower, which I've made into a doghouse for Max and Floyd, the Malamute-Sheltie stray that took up with me in Kansas. Ten feet down the hill behind the cabin, the Chattahoochee National Forest begins its broad stretch toward Tennessee. A few miles south lies the old gold-mining town of Dahlonega.

The cabin sits alone near the crest of a solitary hill in the Yahoola Valley, gathered in among white pines and scarlet oaks, mosses and ferns, mountain laurel and rhododendron. Across the driveway the crest forms a knoll, and on the knoll is a clearing with a view of the ridge of mountains to the north and a constant breeze. Crisscrossed with the trails of deer and dogs, the knoll has an ancient quality, like ruins. Perhaps there are Yunwi Tsunsdi here, Cherokee spirit people like fairies, who love music and magic and whose hair grows almost to the ground. But this is charmed land, U.J. says.

Now U.J. is showing me how the door to the screened porch won't close unless I pull up on it. Then we go down for the storage room tour. "This is the hot water heater," he says, pointing. "But there's nothing you need to do with that."

"That's a good thing."

"This is the heat pump. But there's nothing you need to do with that."

"Good. All this stuff looks alike to me."

"This is the water filter. Flush it twice a week." He shows me how.

"I can do that."

Then he lifts the lid of his toolbox to show me where I can find tools I might need. His tools lie in perfect formation, like little soldiers. "I haven't put up the pegboard yet," he explains.

We head around the corner to the outdoor shower, then upstairs to the den. Finally U.J. takes a last look around and starts for the door. "Oh," he says, turning back to me. "There's a hole by the front gate you have to watch out for. My insurance company told me to tell people about it."

"How thoughtful."

"When you close the gate, you have to lift up and shove," he says, pantomiming. "You'll think you can't do it, but you can."

"I can do it." (I say this more forcefully than is necessary.)

"A last hint," he says as he closes the kitchen door. "If you hold the door with this hand—" (he shows me) "—you won't skin your knuckles." He grins, and his blue eyes twinkle. I remember this grin from my childhood, and it makes me laugh. How extraordinary, I'm thinking, to feel taken care of.

Trail Head: White Pine Cabin

It is Aunt Helen and Uncle Johnny who belong to this place, not I. I've only come visiting, while I work through the next few paragraphs of my life. The furnishings are all theirs: their finds, their inheritance, their handiwork. A branch propped across a window holds a bird's nest from A.H.'s walks; the husk of a giant cicada clings to the screen. She has arranged stones from the creek and flakes of mica in a white dish, dried grasses in a mug, violet leaves around a pinecone in a corner of the bathroom shelf. U.J.'s father built these bookcases. U.J. himself built the cupboards.

But I am establishing a presence here. Pushed up against the west wall, Grandmama's card table now holds my computer and half an acorn I picked up in the driveway, magenta in the middle. A cup warmer for my coffee is within easy reach of the keyboard. The wind chime I made of seashells and driftwood hangs from the porch eaves, its music exotic in the pine-scented breezes, reminding me of salt air and beaches.

Now I've thrown open the doors and windows, trying to shake off the bleak Kansas winter I've left behind. Dusk has fallen. I can hear the creek rushing southward at the foot of the hill. Across the valley I can just make out a wiry thread of trail winding into the mountains. Evening brings a chill, the occasional call of a crow or a dog.

"To endure oneself may be
the hardest task in the universe."
FRANK HERBERT, *Dune Messiah*

CROWS

North-Georgia winters are perverse: one day you're
wearing sandals, the next you're iced in for a week. Today
was warm enough for shorts.

I opened the doors and windows and went out on the
front porch with my coffee. The light was good for hiking
because the sky was overcast, which cut the glare, and I
thought I smelled rain in the gusts of wind bringing damp
air up from the Gulf.

Behind the cabin, a path through the woods leads to an
old road that curls up into the mountains. The road is
closed and not maintained, but I can walk it now that the
summer undergrowth is gone, and I wanted to find out
where it went. So I finished my coffee and took off with
the dogs, and we crashed like bears over the dried leaves
that covered the forest floor.

The road started at an easy climb, but the day was humid and I was soon damp with perspiration, so I hung my lavender sweater on a branch where I'd be sure to see it on the way back down. I walked along trying to identify the foliage unfamiliar to my flatlander's eyes—partridge-berry, galax, Joe-Pye weed—when the dogs darted down a trail to the left.

The trail quickly broadened into a wide, high ledge—obviously a mecca for hunters, who'd left beer cans and shell casings scattered around. Blackberry vines lay in tangles down the slope, and through the pines to the north I could make out the sharp peak of Black Mountain. If I climbed straight down from here, I thought, I'd probably find U.J.'s spring. Pine seedlings blocked the trail farther down, so I backtracked and hiked on up the forest road.

The land dropped hundreds of feet on my right and rose as high again on my left, the road rising slowly, skirting the side of the mountain. I wondered what it had been used for—perhaps for mica mining. Mica was strewn all over the ground in these mountains, as though a thousand mirrors had broken here.

Another steep trail to the left led me through a stand of laurel to an overlook and then ended—another favorite spot for hunters. Again I backtracked to the main road.

It wasn't long before I felt the wind shift. The scent of rain I'd noticed in the morning disappeared, and the temperature dropped. The dogs were frisky, but I was soon cold, so for the third time on this hike I turned around, deciding to try again another day. On the way back down, I rounded a curve and blundered into my lavender sweater, stretched out like a scarecrow on a pine branch jutting over the road. It scared me. For an instant I had the weirdest feeling I'd come face to face with myself.

Back at the cabin, I decided to try an exercise in expanding aural awareness I had learned from a book by Georgia outdoorsman Charlie Elliott. Charlie would sit silently for thirty minutes and write down every sound he heard. What he noticed right away, he said, was that the loudest sound claimed all his attention. He had to train himself to hear what lay beneath. It helped to turn on a tape recorder, he said, because when he played it back and compared it to his list, he could find out what he'd missed.

I didn't have a tape recorder, so my notepad would have to do. But this is an advantage of living alone: you're the only one you have to check with. If you can't decide which jeans to wear, you can just look in the mirror. "I think all my jeans have shrunk," you can say, trying on all your jeans (ignoring the extra five pounds you're wearing).

"Oh, definitely," comes the reply. "Probably those dryers at the Laundromat."

If you don't think you'll like what you see in the mirror, you don't have to look.

Now I made a cup of tea and brought it out to my reading chair on the screened porch and for seven minutes, because it was too cold to stay longer, I listed everything I heard:

9

a light wind
dead leaves that haven't fallen, make ticking sounds
     when the wind blows
car way off in the distance
bird with high-pitched, squeaking song (what bird?)
crow cawing
a single step, or something falling, on the dry leaves
     down the hill
fly hitting against the screen
dogs moving around
myself moving around
man calling to someone down the hill
wind picking up

Charlie Elliott once confessed that when he played back his tape, he was astonished to learn that he'd missed a whole flock of crows. Never mind that when I read my list back I hadn't recorded myself breathing, or picking up my cup of tea or setting it down or sipping or swallowing, hadn't even noticed my pencil scratching against the page as I wrote. Surely I'd never have missed a flock of crows!

...the weightlessness of us as things around begin to shift...
THE INDIGO GIRLS
"Everything in its Own Time"

"no big deal"

The cold was blistering. The trees that hemmed in White Pine Cabin creaked and thrashed in the blasts of icy wind that sailed down from the mountains. When I let in my friend Mark, who had come to visit, my thin-skinned little gray dog Max was sitting straight up outside the door, shivering. Now he was curled in a tight ball on his blanket near the futon, sound asleep. Floyd with his thick coat and Malamute temperament watched out from the porch, content with the weather.

An expert in primitive survival skills, Mark was a local naturalist who was schooling me in the ways of bear and black birch, poison ivy and jewel weed. But today I'd asked him over for a different reason. I wanted his calm, detached perspective on the nightmare I'd just been through in graduate school. I was going back next month to finish out the academic year, and I was looking for some wisdom to use as a charm to banish the bad dream that haunted me. Never mind that I'd told the story dozens of times, collected charms from friends to professors to priests. The spell was still on me.

I'd prepared Mark well. "It was a nightmare!" I'd exclaimed, giving him none of the details. "Devastating! I'll never get over it!"

Now Mark sat quietly on the futon, his bad back straight against the hard cushion, his hands in his lap. I bustled around the cabin, chattering on about the cold, and turned up the heat.

Mark didn't drink coffee, so I got him a glass of water and poured coffee for myself, dumped in some cream, and sat down in a canvas chair facing him. Our knees almost touched in that tiny space, and I wondered if he sensed the tension in my body as I started talking.

It was the end of a Kansas August as hot and humid as any South Georgia summer, and I had just spent four hours in the pressure cooker that graduate English departments call "comps," the oral comprehensive exams that determine whether a student is qualified to defend his dissertation and receive a Ph.D.

I paced the hall outside the door where my professors were conferring. I knew I'd passed. I hadn't handled the exams well, but failure was impossible. I was an exemplary student. I'd never even taken a summer off. Mine were spent, if not in classes, then reading ahead for the coming semester, or writing. I'd earned a prestigious four-year fellowship that provided a generous living stipend, tuition, and expense money. I'd just published my second book, was often invited to speak to audiences and writers all over the country, and maintained a stint as a public radio commentator. I did not flunk exams.

But ten minutes had gone by. What was taking so long? I moved down the hall, not wanting to overhear. *Maybe they're trying to decide whether to award me honors,* I thought.

It was medieval torture, going through comps. Where did they come up with those questions?

"I strongly advise you to attend regular meetings with your professors before your exams," the graduate coordinator had advised me more than once. "You may not think it's necessary, but I guarantee it will give you a better idea what kinds of questions to expect."

"Surely by now I know how to study for a test," I'd said smugly. "What could they possibly tell me that they haven't already said? I'd rather focus on my writing."

Twenty minutes. What on earth was happening in there? They knew what a good student I was.

Twenty-five minutes.

It wasn't all that important, I told myself. A doctorate had never been my dream anyway. Sure, school had been an invaluable resource, provided me time and intellectual resources for writing. But I didn't *have* to have a Ph.D. I had no interest in teaching. I could have been at A.H.'s cabin right then, working on the next book. I could have walked away any time I wanted to. Any old time.

Thirty minutes. Okay, now I was mad. How long could it take to say yes or no?

Well...not no, of course.

All those people. My parents. My benefactors. My department. My friends. I was a graduate fellow, for heaven's sake. We didn't flunk out of graduate school!

But there was the door opening. At last.

The committee poured out. Two professors glanced at me and headed in the opposite direction. I thought of the jury who refused to make eye contact with the defendant they'd just voted to convict. A third professor smiled, told me my exam chair, Beth, would talk to me, and sailed by. I watched her until she rounded the corner at the end of the hall, but she never looked back.

That was odd, I thought.

Beth was last. She put her arm around me and walked me inside the room, told me to sit, and closed the door. She sat facing me and took my hands. She looked me in the eye. I'd known Beth since I'd arrived at the university. She was a friend.

"Well, dear one," she said, her eyes tearing, "I'm afraid the news is not good."

"What do you mean, 'not good'?" (There were three parts to the exam. Maybe I'd not done well on one of them.)

"I'm afraid your committee has decided that you did not pass your exams."

I sat back in my chair. "Beth."

She shook her head. "I'm so sorry. I know you're terribly disappointed."

Terribly disappointed? "None of it? Not one part?"

"I'm afraid not."

I stared at her. "No."

There was a silence.

"I can't believe it," I said.

"Frankly, Amy, neither can we."

The irrevocability of her words hit me then, and I buried my head in my hands and sobbed. "All those years!" I said. "All that work!"

She handed me a Kleenex. "It's going to be all right, Amy. You can get through this."

"How can it be all right? *I've flunked my comps!*"

At White Pine Cabin, Mark sat silent, watching me. I had shifted away from him and was kicking my crossed leg up and down. I squeezed my elbows into my sides, clutching my empty mug. "Can you imagine?" I said. "I was destroyed. I was no longer a person."

"It must have been terrible for you," Mark said. "What did you do?"

"I couldn't stop crying at first, I was so *humiliated.* But eventually I pulled myself together. My mind started grinding through details, and I started asking questions."

I took a shaky breath and looked up at Beth. I imagined a big red "F" scrawled across my perfect academic record...no, scrawled across my life. I have failed life, I thought. How do you fail life? "So what happens now?" I said. "Can I do anything? What can I do?"

"There is something you can do," Beth said, "if you're willing to do the work. But it's not going to be easy."

She explained that, in accordance with department policy, my committee could test me again. If I'd go back

15

and re-read the dozens of books on my study list and meet with each of my professors every week for the rest of the semester, I could retake the exams in November. If I passed, my record would remain unblemished. "These exams are tough, Amy," Beth said. "This happens sometimes."

"No it doesn't," I said. "Not to me."

The bottom line, Beth explained, was that, because I'd been outside the academic environment since finishing my coursework, writing my book, and because I'd not stayed in contact with my professors as I'd studied for my comps over the last year, my scholarship had suffered. Despite my brave words to the graduate coordinator, I had forgotten how to study.

This was absolutely true. I could hardly stand to admit it, but I'd suspected it all along. Yet somehow I'd stubbornly made up my mind that, if all else failed, my innate creativity would rescue me, as it had always done.

"This strategy is ineffectual if you have not done the work," I said to Mark, getting up to pour myself more coffee. I stirred in too much cream and blew my nose on a paper towel. Outside, the wind howled in the eaves and shoved branches around. My wind chime was loud on the porch. I wondered if the shells would crack.

Mark moved a little to ease his back. Max was still curled on his blanket. The cabin was chilly, and the hot mug felt good in my hands.

The thought of four months under the strain of Beth's notoriously difficult study regimen felt like a yoke across my shoulders. And yet how could I turn down this second chance, after all my years in school plus the enormous investments so many others had made? Walking away might have sounded good while I was bent under the weight of my shame, but my instincts told me that a day would come when I'd regret having given up. So I accepted Beth's conditions and set my mind to begin again.

But my pride was shattered, and pride having always made up a large share of my ego, by the time I returned to the crude, unwelcoming house I lived in, I felt dispossessed. My life seemed unfamiliar. I was crushed. Embarrassed. Afraid. Who are you, after all, when the dream of yourself that you've built your life around suddenly collapses under the weight of your error? It's like waking up in a strange room not knowing who you are and having to decipher the world all over again, one minute, one object, one unfamiliar face at a time.

I called my mom, dad, sister, best friend, even Aunt Helen and Uncle Johnny, and told them what had happened. It was awful. Then I drank a shot of vodka and called my professors to discuss the weaknesses in my performance. I set up appointment times. As I talked to them, I realized with terrible clarity the mistake I'd made not keeping in touch with them all along.

I started reading from morning to midnight. I analyzed theme, image, intent, influence, made page after page of notes. I didn't know whether I was afraid to stop, or afraid not to. Sometimes I enjoyed the work, but I didn't like to admit that. I preferred the days when I resented it, so I could be bitter. *Who needs academics?* I'd think. *I'm just doing this because I'll regret quitting.*

And always, every minute, I longed to escape, run away to Georgia, get on with my "real" life. It was so hard to acknowledge that it was *all* my real life.

The new exams were scheduled for late November. The day was clear, the sky an impossible shade of blue, so bright and deep and clean it seemed some cartoonist had filled it in by hand, laying the color down hard against the straw-colored fields and the dark roofs of houses, the shimmering cottonwoods, the white trunks of the sycamores.

Yet all morning I'd felt terrible, like I was waiting to learn the results of a cancer biopsy. I knew I could walk into that room and leave it feeling even worse than when I'd arrived.

At last the time came for me to leave for the university. I'd put away my notes long before, too nervous to concentrate. I gathered up a brown stone I liked to hold in my hand and some photos of White Pine Cabin that A.H. had sent me and drove to school. On the way, I bought a triple cappuccino, along with a handful of Ghiardelli chocolates to pass around to my professors. I prayed they wouldn't be grim and serious, that they would laugh and look me in the eye.

The exams lasted hours and the questions were hard. I wasn't a star. I couldn't remember answers, didn't know answers, didn't articulate well the answers I did know. I didn't earn honors. But I passed my comps.

Mark had barely moved for two hours. I sat on the edge of my chair trembling with emotion and strung out from all that coffee. The wind had died, and now the only sound was the low hum of the refrigerator. "I'm wrecked! Totally caved in!" I blurted into the silence. It was an accusation. "I'll never be the same!"

Mark shook his head slowly, his expression serious.

I frowned. "What?"

"Amy. That's not a story of failure. Don't you see?"

"Of course it is. What do you mean?"

"That's a story of triumph."

I blinked. "Huh?"

"That's a comeback story."

For a minute I just couldn't see it, though I was desperate to grasp his meaning. Then all at once it hit me, and the tentacled monster that had been wrapped around my stomach for months finally let me go.

A baby ring-neck snake was crossing the driveway when I almost stepped on it. I crouched down to catch it. I've always wanted to catch a wild snake in my hands, just to prove to myself I wasn't afraid. This one was barely four inches long, slender, glossy black, with a thin ring of yellow around its neck. I put my hand on it to stop it, but it squirmed away. Every time I picked it up, it moved so violently that I got scared and dropped it.

Thoreau wrote that before any real progress can be made, we have to unlearn and learn anew what we thought we knew before. The Zen masters say that it is life to be

19

able to live comfortably among uncertainties. In my experience, identities are always uncertainties, and it can kill you to catch one like a snake and keep it trapped between your fingers.

mountain dogs

Max challenged the neighborhood bully as soon as we moved in. Some orange dog, the color of pine straw, with a definite Bullmastiff in its past and a head that would have made more sense on a buffalo. Max strutted up and stuck his nose in the orange dog's face. The orange dog went away. Max is nothing if not cheeky.

Max is a dignified little dog. He does not like to be held. If I pick him up, his legs go stiff and straight as boards. If I turn him on his back, his legs stick up like table legs. If I gush compliments at him, he stands expressionless as a Buckingham palace guard, except his tail might move. Slightly.

Max does love attention, but he asks for it in his own time, like a fussy cat. If I ignore him, he sits at my feet and stares up at me until I pat his head, his one flopped-over ear lending a quaint charm to his self-possession. Max knows his own mind, is what it is. He knows mine, too, which is more than I know and is unsettling in a dog.

Max does nothing unnecessary if he can help it. He finds rain inconvenient. When I open the door in the morning to let him out, if he sees rain, he just blinks at it. After a minute, he turns around and goes back to his blanket.

Max is also a practical dog. He's not noisy unless noise is called for, and he's certainly never been a howler. When Floyd starts howling, Max looks around and sniffs, as if such lack of modesty were just *too* crass. Floyd has no modesty. He howls at everything: wind, cars, coyotes, people. Sometimes he howls for no reason at all.

But lately I think some of Floyd's enthusiasm has worn off on Max, because the other night I'm sure I heard Max trying to howl. At first I didn't know what it was, that sound, it was such a small sound, a kind of embarrassed low *mmmf* next to Floyd's high-pitched yipping, and I could barely hear it on the front porch. When I went out to investigate, Max glanced at me sideways, as though he was wondering whether I'd seen him do it or not.

I took Floyd in when he showed up one winter at the House of Steps in Kansas. He was a wraith of a dog then, colorless and half-starved and skittish. Now he has thick golden fur and a face like a Malamute, a coat like a Sheltie, and more life in him than all my five-year-old cousins put together. When Floyd plunges into water, which he loves like a Labrador, he dashes back out at a full run and shakes himself so hard his whole back end comes off the ground and his legs fly out in all directions. Floyd is an energetic dog.

Floyd loves the mountains. He likes the creeks in particular, where he can stand up to his neck in the cold water and cool off under that fur coat of his, and he likes long walks in the woods. He likes to see where the deer trails go. If he gets too far ahead of me, he flops down across the path and waits for me to catch up. When I reach him he gives me an exasperated look, then jumps up and runs off again.

Max has no time for this nonsense. He is busy on patrol.

Floyd loves to run. His favorite game is race-the-car. He likes to charge down the driveway and burst out into the road in front of me, weaving like a drunkard until I can get around him. He runs beside me until he gets tired, then stands in the road and watches until I'm out of sight. It reminds me of my dad, who when I drive away after visiting him also stands in the road and watches until I'm out of sight. He's got this lost, hopeful look, like he wishes I'd turn around and come back and get him.

Max used to chase the car when he was younger, but he is too mature for that now.

Floyd is afraid of most people. He waits a long time before he lets anyone touch him. He's especially afraid of men. Perhaps a man kept Floyd locked up when he was a puppy, because now he won't come inside unless he knows he can get out. If I close the door behind him, he gets this panicky look, like a trapped bird. As soon as I open the

23

door again, he goes through it like a shot, then turns around and barks for me to come out where he is.

Floyd was a lost dog. I collect lost dogs like lint. Even when I try to avoid them, they search me out and attach themselves. On New Year's Day in A.H.'s neighborhood, a frail-looking tall brown bony dog with undeniable eyes started following me around when I went for a walk. He followed me all the way back to A.H.'s, but when I went into the house to get him some food, she rescued me and sent him away.

Now it seems I have collected that big orange neighborhood bully dog. He was sitting on the porch like the King of Siam last week when I came back from a hike. I had already noticed the dog food mysteriously disappearing.

I called the orange dog Ono at first, because that was how I felt every time I saw him coming. Lord knows I didn't need another dog. Then I decided the humor would get tired, so now I call him Sam. Sam from Siam. I asked around, but nobody's claiming him.

Here's what Sam is mainly: massive. But he's a sweet-natured dog, mild-mannered and courteous, not a bully at all, and he never gets rattled. He's like a large orange monk. He eats more than a monk, though.

I used to collect lost people. They were all men. They were sometimes damaged when I found them. But then so was I.

Sometimes we were both all right at first but after a while we were both damaged. I don't know why that was.

It's not as easy to fix a damaged person as it is to fix a damaged dog. If a dog gets sick, you can take him to the vet. The vet gives you some medicine, you give the medicine to the dog, the dog gets well. Or not.

You can yell at a dog, push him out of the way, ignore him, forget to feed him, put him outside in the summertime until he goes to lie hot and panting under the porch, or leave him by himself all day while you go to town. Still when you get home he runs up to you and wags his tail, wanting to be petted, giving you in full measure whatever you neglected to give—whether you ask for it or not.

Anyone can be somebody's fool.
NANCI GRIFFITH, *Little Love Affairs*

rewriting Ulysses

I thought I'd left the cowboys in Kansas, but driving down to the Wal-Mart in Dahlonega on Sunday I saw a sign advertising a horse show and passed a caravan of custom-built pickups pulling air-conditioned horse trailers around the S-curves toward a local resort called R-Ranch. I got behind three vaqueros in a Mercury Cougar, their hats all I could see except for the bucking bronco swinging on a chain from the rearview mirror. I was listening to country music at the time, on a station with a D.J. who can call himself George Mason-Dixon without cracking up. When I tuned in NPR, darned if there wasn't Jerry Alfred and the Medicine Beat singing *nendaa, nendaa,* go back, go back, go back to your roots.

In graduate school I wrote an essay about my most recent torrid love affair, which is now over, which nearly killed me. I called the essay "Ulysses Sails into Port," because I honestly believed he had. I was Penelope, weaving my robe of stories and turning away multitudes of suitors (well, maybe not multitudes) while waiting for Ulysses to return from the wars. Then he did.

The essay was true, the essay was a lie. In hindsight, I should have seen the damage coming. It started like this.

> Three divorces before I turned thirty, not to mention all my other failed romances, had cinched the whole relationship thing for me. Like I'd told my friend Bob: "Bob, I don't do relationships. No offense, but I'm through nursing men through their adolescence. I have too much work to do.
>
> "Besides, I enjoy being by myself. Like, if I want to buy an industrial-size can of pork-and-beans, there's nobody I have to check with first."

The truth was, I was definitely up for a relationship. For months I'd been scanning crowds for the long-haired, blue-eyed blond hero who would recognize me the instant he saw me. I'd never met him, but I was convinced he existed because I'd dreamed about him several times.

Anyway, Bob and I went to breakfast one morning, where...

> ...he had invited his friend George, a dark-eyed, fortyish man with silvering hair, an athlete's build, and teeth just crooked enough to give his handsome face an added share of character.

Okay. So, not blond. Not blue-eyed. Crooked teeth.

So if I was intrigued with George, it was not because he had a great sense of humor or seemed so interesting...

That he was handsome had something to do with it.

A week later, I was walking back to my car from the post office, paging through my new Victoria's Secret catalog, when I ran into George. I cringed, remembering my fat knees and how wide my bottom looked in those old green shorts. "Can you believe how skinny these women are, George?" I said, holding out the catalog. "How do they stay alive like that?"

The subtext here should be clear to all women who do not look like Victoria's Secret models, which is every woman I know.

"One thing I've learned, Amy Blackmarr," George said, "is that when a woman is holding a Victoria's Secret catalog, whatever she says is absolutely right."

He was clever, too. I liked clever men.

"Ha," I said. "That's pretty smart."
When I drove away, I couldn't put George out of my mind for at least twenty minutes...

I hadn't put him out of my mind since I'd met him.

29

...and after that I promised myself I'd forget about him.

A promise as empty as my social life.

On Wednesday, I got this e-mail from Bob: "Has George called you yet?"
"Was he going to call me?" I wrote back. "What on earth for?"

I am shaking my head in shame.

"I think he'll call you."
"You do?"
"You have a lot in common."

30   As if that were the driving motivation here.

The next day, I saw George's truck ahead of me in town. He pulled over and motioned for me to stop. I drove up beside him. He walked to my car and leaned down to look at me. The sun was in his eyes. "Bob tells me you and I have some things in common," he said.
His eyes weren't all that dark, I decided.

I saw little flecks of gold in them.

"Would it be okay if I called you some time?" he said.
I shrugged. "Okay," I said...

(pretending nonchalance.)

On Saturday Bob dropped by the House of Steps for a visit. "Let's call George and ask him to come over," he said. "You haven't really had a chance to talk to him yet." "He probably won't come," I said (wistfully).

The wistful part was true.

Soon we heard George's truck coming down the drive. We watched him climb the deck steps to the sliding glass door, negotiating with my German shepherd, Red, who wasn't sure he wanted to let George in.

Red also hadn't liked the guy who put in the air conditioner, who looked unwashed and emitted a raw smell, like the onions he'd eaten for lunch.

31

I was a mess, sweaty from wrestling with my lawnmower, in cutoffs with my hair in pigtails and my cellulite in full view. Well, he'd have to take me as I was. I took a breath, stuck out my chin, curled up in a deep chair in the den, and tried not to let too much of me show.

Actually I didn't mind my face showing; I sort of liked my face. But I'd as soon have had the rest of me vanish.

"I want to get to know you," I schmoozed as soon as George sat down. "Tell me about yourself. Tell me what you love, what you want, what you dream about." I said these words as if I were a silver-sequined twenty-four-year-old blonde holding a two-olive martini at a cocktail party in Savannah. It was a part I hadn't played in a while, but I still knew the lines by heart. It's in the blood.

This is the part where I started to feel like Blanche DuBois.

Bob and George looked at each other, and the two of them laughed. "You don't waste any time, do you?" George said.

At our age, who has time to waste?

"Well, I just despise chitchat, don't you? It's so dull. I want to talk about important things. So tell me. What's the dream you haven't lived yet, and what's holding you back?"

I'm embarrassed to admit I actually said these things.

George looked at me, then toward the window, as though he were thinking of going out into the open space of the yard, and didn't say anything for a long time. Bob, surprised by the sudden intensity between his friends, became the soundless observer, and I remembered a line from Yeats, where friends sit grown quiet at the name of love.

Oh, Lord.

After a while, George turned back to me. "Why do you want to know?" he said.

This was not exactly the response I was expecting.

"Well…it tells me a lot about you."

"How do I know you're not just a writer after a story?" George said.

Good grief. Did he think he was that important? Why not just answer the question, chat a little? Why was he suspicious? These questions occurred to me in a flash. A herald might as well have rushed into the room waving a red flag. But I plunged on.

> "Well, you don't. But I'm not after a story. I mean, this isn't the kind of thing I write about."

Well…not usually.

> He didn't talk much, and for long periods while Bob and I chatted George sat quiet, watching me, his hands folded in his lap, one long faded-jeans-clad leg crossed casually over the other, while I carried on like a debutante. But sometimes he'd throw back his head and laugh, or make some wise remark, and his words, infrequent as they were, always seemed to get at something essential in me, seemed to burn through to a part of myself I'd shoved out of sight like a neglected doll. It wasn't his intention: I could see that. It was just how he was, unobtrusive but, still, entirely present.

33

It was all a romantic dream, of course. Whitewash, an illusion, my imagination. If I heard George's words at my core, it was only because I wanted them to strike me there. He did not toss his thoughts into the air like I did, to be reached for and played with and tossed back and laughed over. I learned later that his spare comments, carefully worded, only marked a long-nurtured caution that masqueraded as serenity.

Later still, after I'd settled in here at White Pine Cabin, I was curled up on the futon on a cold night reading Jane Austen's *Persuasion* and ran across these lines: "Mr. Elliot was rational, discreet, polished—but he was not open.... She prized the frank, the openhearted, the eager character beyond all others. Warmth and enthusiasm did captivate her still. She felt that she could so much more depend upon the sincerity of those who sometimes looked or said a careless or a hasty thing, than of those whose presence of mind never varied, whose tongue never slipped."

But with George, I'd been determined to believe in gods, in myth, in fate and drama and romance.

There was a serenity about him that was familiar to me, one that beneath my frenzied girlishness I also knew, and treasured. It was a quality of attention that had come to me from living alone, but I'd lost touch with it since leaving my hermit's life at my granddaddy's South-Georgia cabin for this tall house on unfamiliar ground a thousand miles from everything I thought I knew. In the chaos of the move, in the disturbance of settling down in strange territory, the quietness of spirit I'd cultivated had disappeared inside me out of reach, and I yearned for it—and yearned, I realized now, to be close to someone who understood such things.

True. I had lost my balance with the loss of Pop's farm. And yet, in hindsight, my attraction to George wasn't *all* so deep and spiritual as that. Sure, I wanted to believe he had some secret wisdom that would return my inner peace to me. What I also wanted could be read about in any paperback novel with a bursting bodice and Manly Hero on the cover. But I grew up where it was decidedly déclassé to admit you knew what was inside a man's pants.

> When Bob went home late that night and left us alone, I felt a sudden sadness. "Sometimes I long—" I said, and stopped, not knowing how to finish.

Pooh. I knew exactly how to finish. "Sometimes I long to be trapped with a Manly Hero in a snowbound cabin with the wind howling outside and no cell phone in sight."

35

> "Sometimes I long—" Again I stopped. I looked at George.

What a minx I was!

> "What do you long for?" he said, his voice soft.
> "Company," I said finally.

Well, there was something to that, too.

> He touched my hand. After a while, we said goodbye, and he went home. Didn't say he'd drop by again, didn't say he'd call me later.

I was hooked. I stopped eating, smoked cigarettes, played love songs on the stereo and paced the floor. My old tricks hadn't worked. I couldn't figure it out. I thought I'd said the right words, worked the right spells to awaken his interest, but he hadn't fallen for me. He hadn't responded to my Womanhood in the customary way, hadn't played his part and flirted back.

Then it hit me. I couldn't play my old role with this man. This was not a tragedy. I couldn't be the *femme fatale*.

But I did, it was, and I was. Only the victim was not the one I expected.

It was like going back to read an essay that had never been quite right, and somehow in the process of living I'd figured out what was wrong with it. My God. I saw myself truly, and I was out of my time. I wasn't Penelope; I was Blanche DuBois in dim light, wrapping the enchanting young woman I had once been around an aging, lonesome Southern girl who clung to a coquette's guile though her looks had made her irrelevant. I imagined myself at sixty, still acting seventeen and making a fool of myself. I felt my identity sloughing off like dead skin, and I had no idea what to make of the raw woman underneath.

Hindsight is a dangerous thing, like a lightning-struck tree about to fall. I'm a few inches over five feet, blue-eyed, and blonde, a petite female reflection of the hero I envisioned in my dreams. I've always wanted to be tall, so my clothes would hang on me as beautifully as my tall sister's hang on her and so I wouldn't have to hem up all my pants. Most of the men in my life have been tall.

I adored George. I thought he was going to be with me forever. But George was never Ulysses, and the signs had been there all along: that outward calm and the reticence I chose to see as wisdom were really just George calculating consequences.

And I wasn't blameless, either. I played games from the start, and I exacted revenge in my cruel little ways. When George finally left, I shouldn't have been so surprised.

Today the wind is up, worrying the leaves of the red oak I can see through the window above my computer. To the south are pines and a dogwood; in front of those, a maple; beyond them, forest. From where I sit, everything I see is consumed by forest, and all of it is moving.

37

a sharp tooth

Today I hiked back up the forest road and found oak leaves still scarlet even in January. Sugar maple leaves with as many bright greens and yellows and crimsons as if an artist had spilled her paints.

Most startling: orange and yellow tulip tree leaves as broad as Japanese fans. *Liriodendron tulipifera.* Seems a grand enough name for such a tree. One tulip tree in North Carolina was over a thousand years old when it burned in 1935. Two hundred feet tall, eleven feet in diameter. You couldn't get your arms around it.

I was standing at the edge of the road looking into the valley far below, when on a ledge beneath me I spied a blue bush growing under a white pine tree. The bush wasn't tall; rather, each thickly needled branch was growing straight out of the ground, about the length of my arm. It was such a strange shade of blue, I wondered if someone had brought it from Canada or Alaska. It certainly wasn't a native.

I slid down to the ledge and crawled to the bush. The needles were cold and smooth to touch. I tried to pull a few off the branch, but they held fast. The wood was stiff and rust-colored and had a twisted, almost braided look. I couldn't detect any scent. How peculiar. I'd never seen such a bush.

Then I noticed something glittering. Silver.

I touched it. *Tinsel.* So that was it.

Now why would anybody drag an artificial Christmas tree a mile into the forest and leave it? When I got over being annoyed, the irony made me laugh. Still I couldn't help thinking of a line from Frank Herbert's *Dune* novels, about how the highest function of ecology is understanding consequences.

I climbed back up to the forest road and went on. After half a mile, the road leveled off at a high point, where water trickled down a moss-covered rock face overgrown with mountain laurel, ferns, and galax, its heart-shaped leaves now deep red. The water formed a pool so clear and still that the pale yellow leaves lining the bottom might have been painted under glass. Even though I knew better, I was tempted to drink from it—but then the dogs tore around the corner and plunged into it and my reflecting pool became a mud puddle. After a few minutes we went on.

By now the road had narrowed to a grassy track that dropped steeply until it crossed a fast creek, which I followed back up the mountain to a waterfall that cascaded down smooth black rock thirty feet high. The air was cold here, and a ring of stones marked where a campfire had been. The sunlight filtering down through the feathery hemlocks cast the place in a silvery haze, except where a cluster of white beeches stood in a low clearing. The rocks were sea green and sage and shades of gray, and the sky was pale. But the leaves at my feet were jewels: amethysts, rubies, topazes; and the creek water was a cache of scattered diamonds that captured and shone back the last light of waning day. Examining stones, I found a piece of broken bottle, and on the way back to the forest road I retrieved a yogurt cup out of the fork of a tree. I also brought back part of a turtle egg, a bit of white quartz, two acorns, some flakes of mica, and a sharp tooth, which I pushed into the rotten end of the stick I was carrying, pretending it made me a formidable weapon.

41

"1/2 tab about
1 hour before storm

Sam from Siam has defected, flown the coop, gone south. He seemed pleased enough with his meals here at White Pine Cabin, but in the few weeks he boarded with me I could see that he was a wanderer, for he came and went at odd hours and stayed gone for long stretches of time. Perhaps the life here was too small for his expansive tastes.

I liked that orange dog because he seemed fearless, like the mice that took up lodgings with me at the House of Steps along with the snakes, the hummingbirds, and the houseflies.

Late last summer in Kansas on a hot, typically windy day, I was studying for my first attempt at my comps when I decided to stop for a sandwich and a glass of iced tea. I'd propped the kitchen door open with a chair, and when I reached the kitchen I heard a funny sound, like a tiny drum beating against the window. A hummingbird had flown in through the open door. I caught him and put him out again. Birds and things were always getting into that house.

I was tossing the end of a tomato into the trash can when I saw the snake. The part I saw—which didn't include the ends—was at least two feet long and more than an inch thick. Dark gray and filmy, it lay motionless on the brick floor cooling its blood, I guessed, on that hot Midwestern afternoon. I could see its tail curled around a caster on my rolling cabinet. No rattles: thank heaven for that. Its head was...I couldn't see its head, but it must be somewhere between the box of mouse poison and the sink drain.

It *looked* like a black rat snake, but I wasn't sure. I watched it, wondering what to do. I thought of getting my walking stick from upstairs and herding the snake out the door, but it was so still, I wasn't even sure it was alive. I touched it with my toe and jumped away. It dented! Then I realized. It was only the skin.

I had a brainstorm then. Maybe this snakeskin could help me get a leg up on the mice, who came and went with abandon wherever I lived—especially, because of the holes in the walls, at *this* house.

I retrieved what I could of the skin (the head and tail broke off but I got the middle) and for a few days kept it near my computer, where the mice had been taking late-night saunters around the mouse pad. But when I began to notice a funky odor, I moved the skin back to the kitchen. There I stretched it along the window ledge beside the sink. Surely those silly mice would mistake this shell for what belonged inside it and either collapse with heart failure or run away forever.

For a week, this strategy seemed to be working. I saw no mice in the house, nor any sign that they'd been out on extended sightseeing expeditions around the kitchen. On top of the stove, along the counter near the toaster, I found no tiny torpedoes of mouse evidence to wipe away with the breadcrumbs. The mouse poison looked untouched.

Ha! I thought. *Terrorized by a mere shadow! Scared off by an idea! Ridiculous rodents!*

Then one day I got out the Shop-Vac to suck up the houseflies that liked to cluster in the corners of the kitchen windows, but I got too close to the snakeskin and *schhhlooop!* down the hose it went.

Rats, I thought.

But wait! Wasn't that something skin-like just there, beneath the window? Yes! Crumbled bits of snakeskin were scattered like confetti all along the window ledge. They trailed off toward the potted oregano...where snakeskin-colored mouse torpedoes lay bunched in clues of casual profusion.

Fear is a mind-killer. Max is not afraid of big orange dogs or ear-shredding bobcats or even Mack trucks but he is reduced to drooling madness by thunder. One faint rumble in the distance and he materializes on the cabin porch all a-tremble, his eyes as large as UFOs and his heartbeat like a drum roll. I let him in and he sits like a statue at my feet and stares at me in utter panic, like a condemned criminal

45

heading for the gallows, like a tortured soul at the threshold of hell, pleading for absolution. It's that bad.

He thinks I can turn the thunder off. "Please, Max, you've got to stop that!" I tell him. "I can't stand it." Honestly, it's heartrending. When I go to bed, good old Max, who has always been too independent to sleep on the bed with me, climbs up and tries to lie down on my head. Whatever position I end up in, he wants to be *in* my *face*—this from one who at any other time contracts rigor mortis when you try to hold him. When lightning flashes, his eyes bug out, and his tongue hangs down, and he drools and pants and pants and drools until my pillow is wet and the whole room smells like dog breath.

One day in desperation I went to the vet and got Max some doggie Valium. Twelve for a dollar. Powerful stuff. "He goes crazy," I explained. "I'm afraid his heart's going to blow up."

"I should warn you," said the vet. "In a few cases, these pills can actually make a dog worse."

"Not possible," I said. "If he got any worse he'd be dead."

"Let's hope not," said the vet.

"1/2 tab about 1 hr before storm," read the label.

"Hmm," I said. "But how—?"

"They take a little while to work," explained the vet.

Last night the dogs and I went through our first monster North-Georgia thunderstorm. Thunder crashed and slammed around the mountains like a maniac. Floyd was unruffled. He hid out in the red-clay cave he has dug under the cabin, preferring that rustic setting to the outdoor shower room where I put his blanket. The red clay turns his white fur orange, but he's not the sort of dog who minds.

But one clap of thunder and Max's whole body was like a stricken cymbal. I brought him indoors and gave him a pill, but as far as I could see all that did was make him drunk. He wandered around all over the place. He went into the shower and came back out. He went under the sink and came back out. He made a racket walking on some papers I had spread on the futon. He was trying to figure out how to get up to the loft, where I was busy not-sleeping.

Finally I pulled myself to the railing and peered down at him from my pallet. "Max, old man," I said, "people have to sleep." The rain was hammering the windows, the thunder like a war. He was so miserable. It was awful. He was just stuck there in the being-scared, waiting for me, his betrayer, to turn off the storm. He looked up at me and whimpered.

I got out of bed, climbed down the ladder, and put my arms around him. "Max, buddy," I said. "Remember the snakeskin. If the fear gets to be too much for you, just *eat* it."

But Max would have none of my advice. When lightning finally blasted a tree near the cabin he dove under the card table, and that's where he stayed until the storm blew east to bother Carolina dogs next morning.

47

Yahoola i

It's midnight and this old wind is howling and rattling the screen door. Max has taken Floyd exploring, and I'm alone. I've been reading ghost stories. But I'm not scared.

When I was a teenager I checked out all the local haunted houses, cemeteries, and scary movies. I was always on the lookout for evidence of that Other World I was convinced was out there just behind the world I could see. My friends and I would drive into the country on summer nights and sit in the yard at Footsteps, an abandoned house whose walls had been painted blue, someone had told us, to ward off evil spirits. We'd let down the car windows and wait for things to happen. Sometimes they did.

Sometimes we'd walk up the steps and cross the porch and tiptoe around in the house, feeling our way up the rotting staircase to the second floor, trying to prove something. Always at night, in the pitch-black dark or the moonlight dark. And we would see what we wanted to see and we would all *believe*. On the way home, swamp ghosts, floating balls of spectral light, would follow our speeding car down the dirt roads.

Ghosts love Savannah, where my sister Kelly lives. Savannah has Confederate soldiers and Civil War hospitals, dead pirates and the spirits of shanghaied boys, lighthouses and widow's walks from which people have thrown themselves. I once went on a ghost tour of Savannah. A guide led me around the squares downtown and stopped in front of the haunted houses and restaurants and museums and told stories of murdered men and voodoo. But that was in broad daylight, so I wasn't all that scared.

Today I picked up these books about North-Georgia ghosts, and found out there are plenty in these mountains—outlaws from gold rush days and murdered Indians and, well, Confederate soldiers. Although up here, plenty of Federals are lying around, too.

What I'm noticing about this mountain cabin tonight is that it's so remote. It's really dark out here when the sun goes down. Noisy when the wind gets up. If a person didn't have a thick skin, this place might get on her nerves. It might get spooky out here. Sometimes I think I hear tinkling sounds way down near the creek, like tiny bells. They harmonize with my wind chimes, the bells' music a counterpoint to the hollow sounds of scallop shells and arcs.

Once in a long while a car with a loud stereo goes by at the bottom of the hill and the vibration comes through the soles of my feet: *bump-BUMP; bump-BUMP*. It reminds me of fifth grade, when we listened to Edgar Allan Poe stories on a record. The telltale heart was under the floorboards: *thump-THUMP; thump-THUMP.*

But that stuff doesn't get the old blood up like it used to. Which is sad, in a way. It must have something to do with turning forty—senses getting numb or something. Right now I'm as calm as an old hound at the master's feet. Really. I'm not scared at all.

Speaking of hounds, my dogs would know before I would if anything was wrong. If anything unwanted came around, I mean. Like bears, for instance.

And Max can see things. He watches invisible people fly around the room. Or maybe invisible dogs. I know they're in the room because his head makes little circles in the air. It's a mystery.

Sometimes I climb up on the knoll and sit in the clearing and contemplate the maze of tiny trails that wind among the trees and beneath the laurel. I imagine they're the paths of the Yunwi Tsunsdi, the Cherokee little people. A woman I know in Kansas had some little people on her land, and she left them presents of jam and jelly in the tops of jars. She said they liked sweet things. But once, she took a little person home with her by accident and had a devil of a time getting him to go back where he came from. Spirit people are everywhere, she used to tell me. You never know where you'll find them.

On this land, a short walk down the road from the bottom of the driveway, two creeks descend from the mountains and converge, forming the headwaters of a creek that flows into Dahlonega. The Cherokee called this place *Yahoola i*, "the place of Yahoola."

Long before the Revolution, Yahoola was a stock trader among the Cherokee villages. He lived at the headwaters of the Yahoola Creek in a small square house made of uncut stone. He tied bells around the necks of his ponies, and as he walked, he sang. People often heard him on the mountain trails.

One day, all the warriors went on a great hunt, and Yahoola went with them—but when it came time to return, Yahoola was gone. For a long time the others waited and searched, but in the end they had no choice but to go home without him. The people grieved for Yahoola. They feared he was dead.

Then one night when the people were at supper, Yahoola suddenly appeared. He had gotten lost on the hunt, he said, but the *Nunne hi*, Cherokee spirit people, had found him and cared for him. Yahoola explained that because he had eaten the food of the immortals, he could no longer live among men. But his longing to see his family had brought him home, and he promised to visit. Then, as suddenly as he had appeared, he vanished.

For a while, Yahoola kept his promise. But eventually he stopped coming, and the Cherokee wondered if the desire of the people to keep Yahoola with them had grown so strong that the *Nunne hi* were offended. Still, people walking along the trail beside Yahoola Creek at night said they could often hear him singing the songs he had liked to sing as he drove his horses across the mountain, and they could hear the crack of his whip and the tinkling of bells.

But they never saw Yahoola nor his horses, even though the sounds passed close by.

After Yahoola disappeared, one of his friends still sang those old songs, but then he died suddenly and the people were afraid to sing them anymore. Finally it was so long since anyone had heard the sounds on the trails that the Cherokees who stayed behind in Georgia thought Yahoola must have gone away, perhaps to the West with the others in 1838.

I didn't know this story the day A.H. came to cut greenery for her house. She didn't know it either, when she took me down to the headwaters of the Yahoola to show me where she thought an old mill had been. We splashed down the middle of the stream, examining the high inner banks. "Right here," she said, pointing to an old hemlock, "you can see where there might have been something once." Embedded in the dirt were the distinct remains of a wall of uncut stone.

Only with the sense that the
world is not solid is it possible to move.
BOB PERELMAN, *a.k.a.*

lost

"*Where do you keep the pushpins?*" I asked the lady at the Dahlonega Wal-Mart. What I really wanted to say was, "Where do you keep the lost dogs?" and I wanted her to answer. "Oh, they're on aisle three by the potato chips," she'd say, and I'd go there and find Max, sitting among the potato chips with a smart look on his face.

I had driven to the Wal-Mart in a panic around noon to pick up some pushpins. I could have done without them, but I wanted an excuse to leave the cabin for a few hours in the hope that when I got back, Max would be back, too. As if he hadn't been gone when I'd gotten up. As if, even though he had been gone, he would have come home, as he always came home, and the long, troubling hours of calling his name and searching the woods and the edges of these mountain roads had never happened. Or if they had happened, it wouldn't have mattered.

Sometime that morning while I was looking for Max I remembered in a kind of moving-picture flash how around daybreak I came barely awake to the sound of the dogs' low growling at intruders—animal or human, I couldn't tell—and then, a few minutes later, a solitary gunshot. "Hunters," I thought, and then I felt a fleeting anguish and murmured, "Oh, Max!" and immediately fell back to sleep. I was tired, having gotten home late the night before from a long trip to Kansas, where I finally received my Ph.D.

A few hours later, the memory of the gunshot buried, I went out to sit on the front porch with my coffee. Floyd was sprawled in the driveway. Max was gone. I called him, but he didn't come. I walked down the drive, listening for his quick trot through the underbrush. Nothing. This was puzzling. When you live with a dog for eight years, you get to know his habits. But maybe his morning rounds were taking him longer than usual.

After an hour, though, and no Max, I was disturbed. I decided to look for him. I called Floyd and we took off down the hill behind the cabin, toward the spring. "Where's Max, Floyd?" I'd say, and Floyd would dash ahead of me through the woods, down a deer trail, down the forest road. But I could find no sign of Max.

I was on the way back to the cabin when with a start I remembered that gunshot. I remembered the instant of anguish I'd felt, and falling back to sleep. I shook my head, refusing the thought of Max dead, and prayed he wasn't lying hurt somewhere, thirsty and in shock. The day was still and hot, the humidity like a pall. A storm was coming. Max hated storms.

Around noon, I gave up looking and drove to town for pushpins. I needed to let myself breathe, relieve the suspense, escape that deep-down alarm that was warning me my life had suddenly gone wrong and there was nothing I could do about it but walk on into the next scene, and the next, while my mind kept grinding through that tangle of memories caught out of bare wakefulness, desperate to sift out some shred that might alter the course I felt was steadily leading me down to that cold *knowing* that lay at the base of my throat like a stone: *I had lost Max.*

So I rushed through the store and asked the lady where to find the pushpins and found them and paid and hurried back, all the while feeling that my leaving the cabin was a kind of betrayal. What if he came home wounded and I was not there to help?

Now, back at the bottom of the driveway, I stopped and listened. I drove up the hill at a crawl, straining to see around the curves, clinging to the belief that Max was back. As I came in sight of the cabin, a tom turkey darted across the drive in front of me, took wing, and landed in the laurel on the knoll. Floyd was sitting placidly on the porch, watching, alone. I was crushed.

I dashed into the cabin, changed into hiking boots, gulped a glass of tea, and grabbed my walking stick, determined to find Max if it took me a week. Max was gray. He blended in. If he were lying down or in a depression, he'd be nearly impossible to see, except that I'd bought him a fluorescent orange collar a few weeks ago. I'd look for the flash of that collar.

Again Floyd and I headed for the spring, crossed it, searched along the creek, came back a different way. The delicate trillium was blossoming. The laurel had burst into bloom all over the mountains. Jacks-in-the-pulpit nodded beside the water, and I crushed dog violets everywhere under my feet. I saw all of spring awakening, even took special note of it, but with a kind of numbness; nothing could claim my attention long. I hiked up the forest road and pushed through the thorny blackberry vines to a place where I'd seen deer hunters in December. Nothing.

I returned to the paved road and walked it again, watching for fluorescent orange among the verbena and honeysuckle and Queen Anne's lace. Nothing.

Presently a sheriff's patrol car came along, and I stopped the deputy and told him my dog had gone missing.

"Lotta things in these woods can get a dog," he said. "Bears, coyotes—"

I shook my head irritably. "Not Max," I said. "He's too smart. Is there some kind of hunting season open? For squirrels, maybe?"

"I don't know. I don't hunt. But a lot of 'em around here does." He paused. "And poaches."

"I was afraid of that."

"It's the only life they know," he added quickly.

I thought he seemed very young. "Do they shoot dogs?" I said, my voice unsteady.

He glanced away, then looked back at me, his expression troubled. "Sometimes."

"Why?"

"They're afraid a dog'll scare the game."

Later that afternoon, tired and sad, I called A.H. and asked her if she would help me look for Max. Together we combed the woods again, sometimes following Floyd. Twice he led us back to the paved road, stopped, and looked around at me. Maybe he sensed what we were doing; maybe he didn't. It didn't really matter anymore. At dark, we gave up. A.H. offered me supper and a bed at her house, but I wanted to stay at the cabin, just in case.

But I knew, as certainly as if someone had shown me Max's body, that he had been the target of that gunshot. I just felt it in my bones. In my years of walks through the woods of South Georgia and eastern Kansas, I'd seen dozens of animals killed that never ended up in cooking pots—coyotes, coons, possums, armadillos, even owls. Charlie Elliott once wrote that while tracking deer he walked up on a hunter whose gun was aimed straight at Charlie's head. If Charlie hadn't spoken, the hunter would have pulled the trigger: he was so prepared to see a deer, he didn't realize that Charlie wasn't one.

59

"I'm afraid the gunshot you heard tells us the story of what happened to Max, Amy," said Mark when I called to ask him about local hunting customs. "And it's a bad story."

"But what about bears? Coyotes?"

"In these woods about the only natural danger to dogs is other dogs. Coyotes will sometimes bother dogs, but that's rare. Bears—that's extremely improbable. Wild dogs can be a threat. But I haven't heard about any packs of wild dogs in these woods recently."

"Oh."

"But around here, Amy, if a hunter sees a dog, even if he knows the dog, he's likely to shoot him."

"I was afraid of that."

"Turkey season is still open. If Max approached a hunter, it would spoil his chances."

"Yeah. That's pretty much what the deputy said."

"Around here there's a kind of unspoken woods ethic," Mark said. "Hunters think dogs shouldn't be allowed to roam freely in the woods."

All I could do was shake my head. I told Mark I hadn't been able to find Max anywhere. "Would they have thrown him down the mountain or something?" I said.

"They probably put something over him. Covering their tracks."

"Right."

There was a silence.

"At least he was free to run," Mark offered.

Two days later.

A ferocious storm blew in the night Max disappeared. I could hardly bear the thought of him lying out there in the woods, terrified by the thunder.

Once today while we were out walking, Floyd sat down at the foot of a pine tree and started barking. He stared up at the branches and wouldn't hush until I went and looked, half expecting to find Max hanging there in some gruesome gesture of warning, like a scene out of the *Blair Witch Project.* But there was nothing. Maybe Max had sprayed the tree a few days ago. Or maybe Floyd just saw a squirrel.

Meanwhile all these awful questions keep running through my mind. Was he running when the bullet hit him? Did he make any sound? Did they take him with them? Did they feel any regret? Did it hurt him? *Is he still alive?* I want to imagine it right, etch the truth into my memory. I want to bring him back and bury him on the knoll, where he made little round nests in the pine straw. But how does one woman with only a stick and a silly fluffy dog search all these square miles of national forest for another dog, dead, gray, thirty pounds on a good day, smart but not quite smart enough?

I keep telling myself: Max is fine. Max doesn't know he's gone. I'm the only one in pain here.

I keep telling myself: It's a risk you take, letting your dogs run, even in the country. Dogs in the country get hit by cars. Dogs in the country get stolen. Dogs in the country get shot by hunters.

And even when I tried, I couldn't keep Max in. He couldn't stand confinement. He had to run. I, of all people, understood that.

Three weeks later.

I've given up hope of finding Max. But I'm keeping a watch out for my sense of humor.

This is something: plants that heal. They grow all over these mountains. You can rub them on your skin to keep the chiggers away. You can eat them for supper. You can boil them for tea and cure diarrhea. Headaches. Motion sickness. Heart sickness. Restoratives, you could call them.

And this is something: a luna moth on the screened porch last night. A turban shell from the Cayman Islands. Beach agates from California. From the creek, quartz so clear I can see through the edges.

Max is gone, and that is a truth. When I think of his small body lying so still, that fluorescent collar flaring like the defiance I knew him for, the contradiction silences me like a furious parent. Even breathing hurts.

But when the hurt subsides—and it always does subside, like a shell sinks to the bottom of the sea—I'm still here. I brush the leaves out of my hair and wash the dirt off my hands, put away my walking stick. I let in the sadness, let it lie in my throat a while, feel it streaming back out. I squat to pet Floyd, and he leans against my thigh. I put my arm around him and lean back into him, a counterbalance to keep from falling.

Antaeus, the son of Terra, the Earth, was a mighty Giant and wrestler, whose strength was invincible so long as he remained in contact with his mother Earth.

BULFINCH'S MYTHOLOGY

above the fall line

It was a Wednesday not long after I lost Max when I set myself the task of climbing a high ridge beside a branch of Walden Creek, and there were moments when I wasn't sure I'd make it back. At times like these a person wishes she'd thought to (1) bring her whistle, (2) eat before leaving home, and (3) tell somebody where she was going.

I wanted to climb the ridge to prepare for the next day, when A.H. and I planned to hike to a part of the Appalachian Trail I thought we could reach from the cabin. According to my topographical map, on the other side of the ridge was a trail that meandered for several miles in view of Black Mountain and led, eventually, to Grassy Gap, where it intersected with the Appalachian Trail. I wanted to make sure the connecting trail was there; it seemed vague from the map and I wasn't sure it was being maintained.

I'd tried to reach the top of the ridge a few days earlier, but I'd started out from the cabin so late that, by the time I reached the creek, I couldn't make the climb and get back to the cabin before sundown. Floyd and I did startle a mythic-sized buck away from the stream, though, a powerful animal with a huge rack, and I tracked him far enough up the ridge for me to learn that the going would be tougher than I'd imagined.

The high point was a thousand feet above the branch and straight up—or straight down, depending on which way you were facing. Even my short climb had been scary, and when I'd turned around to look behind me, the slope dropped out from under me and my feet tingled as though I'd just gotten off a ski lift and was peering over the edge of the mountain to see what I was in for, trying not to over-balance so I wouldn't go down before I was ready, nerving myself to take that plunge that's so steep you can't see the ground under your skis and if you can't remember how to stop, you'd damned well better know how to fall.

So on that Wednesday around four I stowed a liter of water in an old army pack and set out with Floyd to try again. No compass, no map: only my memory of the topo map I'd left taped to the cabin wall. No banana, no apple. I wasn't planning to be gone more than a few hours. The weather was early-spring warm, in the sixties and breezy, perfect for hiking. What was to fear on such a day?

The ridge was a forty-minute hike from the cabin down the forest road that led to the waterfall. At the point where the creek ran along the bottom of the ridge, a narrow trail ambled alongside the water and steadily up for a quarter-mile until it petered out near a pine tree where a hunter kept a deer stand. Around three, I stopped there to drink some water. The ridge formed a steep horseshoe around me, but I had a clear view back the way I'd come, and the mountains immediately behind me were blue-gray and sharp in the cloudless light. Those beyond stretched on for hundreds of miles, gentle reflections of the ones that came before them, their colors softening with the distance.

I hiked to the head of the stream and crossed it. From then on I'd have only my wits until, triumphant, I put my feet down on the trail on the other side of the ridge.

The climb was difficult at first but not daunting, and I was able to stand, grabbing at saplings to pull myself up. Soon, though, I began to wonder if I'd taken on more than I could handle. Maybe I'd been reckless to try this climb alone; for even though I could see the top of the ridge, the grade was soon so steep that I had to drop to all fours to keep from toppling backward. This was no trouble for Floyd, who kept speeding by me like a skateboarder. But falling had always been a particular fear of mine and now I couldn't look back without dizziness, realizing that the slightest miscalculation would send me rolling back down to the branch.

Even so, I knew the fall wouldn't *kill* me—unless I broke my neck on the way down, which seemed unlikely. It wasn't *that* far.

On I went, stubborn as a brickbat, as my maternal grandmother, MaRe (short for Mama Reba), used to say. What was a brickbat, anyway? "Piece of a brick used as a missile." That was me, all right. Hurtling through life like a

65

shot out of a sling and there'd better not be anything in the way. A little afraid—no, a lot afraid—but putting up a bold front in spite of myself, persistent to the end.

And now on this forced march I was determined to prove to myself I could make it up this little piece of ridge. This was nothing, I knew, to seasoned hikers like my friend Nomad, whose agile feet had traveled thousands of miles over the years. He would chuckle at a challenge like this.

But mainly, I wanted to see if my map-reading had been accurate and that connecting trail really was on the other side of the ridge. It was like hunting buried treasure.

So I pulled myself up the mountain, every movement cautious. I stopped often to catch my breath, not from the altitude (in Georgia even the highest mountain isn't five thousand feet), but from the work and the adrenaline. And with my face so close to the ground I saw all kinds of strange things: chunks of white marble embedded with black dots the size of dimes, leggy spiders in profusion, stones heaped beside trees in neat unexplainable piles. Floyd tramped around in the leaves and snooped in the deadfall. I hoped it was still too cool for copperheads.

At last I reached a fallen pine, and I turned around and sat against it to recover my wind. I was twenty feet from the top. I was going to make it. The vista before me lengthened from this height, and I looked out over the miles and, for the moment, put the scary task of going back *down* from my mind.

The trail should be just over the other side of the ridge. When I reached the top I called Floyd and started walking, but I didn't get far before thick stands of laurel blocked every way but back. There had surely never been a path through here.

Frustrated, I climbed back down to the fallen pine and came up on the other side of the laurel. There was a clearing, and sparser undergrowth, and I shouldered my way through it and was heading down the other side when I realized that below me was not a trail but a wide road, or what had once been a road. Now it was more like a ditch, for it hadn't been cleared in years and was rutted and rocky and crisscrossed with blowdown. But it was there, and I had found it, and Black Mountain loomed above me to the north, exactly where it was supposed to be. I was elated. I marked the place where I'd come down the ridge and hiked up the road until the trees thinned, feeling certain the road was passable throughout its length. A mile or so more and, if I'd read the map right, I'd find Grassy Gap and the Appalachian Trail. I turned around and headed for home.

It occurred to me as I contemplated what was sure to be an uncontrollable slide back down the ridge that, rough and rocky as this road was, it was sure to be a better way down the mountain than the way I'd come. I knew (I thought) where it started: off blacktop a half-mile from the cabin. I'd never hiked it because it crossed private property, and the owners had posted a *No Trespassing* sign. But at the moment that seemed a trivial obstacle. Now, feeling pretty smug with my outdoor savvy, I decided to forego the ridge and take the road. Floyd soon disappeared ahead of me.

It wasn't long before I ran into problems. At lower elevations the road was banked five to eight feet on both sides, deeply pitted, and inches deep in dried leaves and rotting vegetation over large loose rocks, a tough hike at any pace. Fallen trees crossed the road every few yards, and if I couldn't get under them I had to climb the banks and go around them, sometimes for long distances because of the knots of impassable laurel, bushy evergreens that multiply like rabbits and form dense hedges. In detouring around the laurel I often lost sight of the road. My sense of direction is not keen, and I worried that I was getting lost. I wished I'd gone down the ridge.

I wanted to go back, but it was too late for that now, because dark was coming on fast, as it will in the mountains, and the temperature was dropping. I had no coat and I'd drunk all my water. I was hungry. I wondered whether this really was the road I remembered from the map, and if it ended where I thought it did or somewhere else, or, if it wasn't the road I thought I was on, how far away from the cabin I might be. I wracked my brain thinking through problems that hadn't even become possibilities yet—even wondered whether I ought to stop there, while I still had enough light to see by, and dig in for the night.

But I kept thinking about a hot shower and warm pajamas. Unwilling to stop until the last minute, I kept going, and just as dark was falling I spied another deer stand. It hadn't been used in a long time, because the seat was rotted and a T-shirt hung from it in rags. Still, it meant people, within walking distance. Then I passed a high chain-link fence surrounded by a second fence of barbed wire, and a NO TRESPASSING sign, and a house, and all at once the road smoothed out and became gravel. I started running and yelling for Floyd, and I kept running until I was standing out of breath on blacktop exactly where I'd expected to be.

So I made it home at last, exhausted and humbled but safe. Floyd went to sleep on the porch, and the Georgia midnight came in peacefully. My body was tired and my knees were shaky, but I knew where I was going, and the next day A.H. and I hiked all the way up to Grassy Gap.

There is a point along the beach where the waves form a miniature waterfall as they recede. You step down into deeper water there, and ocean begins. On the Gulf, it's where Floridians dig sand fleas to boil for chowder. This is the fall line; it's where things fall.

In Georgia, an ancient fall line runs roughly from Columbus in the west, to Macon in the center, to Augusta in the east. Along this line all across the state, rivers plunge over waterfalls where the sea once met the piedmont, and the hills began. Farther north are the Blue Ridge Mountains. To the south, land that once formed the ocean bottom is flat and sandy and strewn with the remains of sea life millions of years gone. I'm a flatlander, used to low ground, and I feel the weight of that old ocean in my bones, holding me to the earth. I don't like high places.

All my life I've clutched stair rails as tightly as MaRe did in her old age, when her bones were brittle and she broke them too easily. Looking down from high places I always feel a kind of dread; even watching cat burglars on TV makes my feet tingle. When I was three, I fell out of bed and broke my collarbone. At six, I drove my bike into a tennis net and somersaulted over the handlebars, which was how Mama found out I was nearsighted. At fourteen, I flew over my handlebars again and took three stitches in my chin. I've fallen off horses, out of canoes, out of favor, in love, and into depression. There are so many ways to fall and, so far as I can tell, no way to avoid them.

Now it's June and early morning in these mountains, and someone phones and wakes me from a deep sleep. "Hey," he says.

"Hey," I say back, too groggy to recognize the voice.

"Did I wake you?"

"No," I lie.

"I want to come cut the grass."

"Okay, U.J." What grass? I wonder.

I hang up and gulp coffee, tidy the cabin, flush the water filter. Is everything the way he wants it? Should I mention that the showerhead drips?

I hike down the drive and open the gate. In less than an hour, he has arrived. Now he's puttering around outside, making preparations, whistling a Sousa march like a virtuoso. He drags a giant Weed Eater out of the storage room. "Don't you winkle on that, now," he tells Floyd.

"Have you had enough coffee this morning, U.J., or can I make you some more?" I want him to be comfortable at his cabin. I watch him from the porch, amused by his industriousness.

"I have everything I need," he says. He marches past me without looking up. He does not come inside. Soon I hear the Weed Eater start up, and I head for my computer.

He's cutting the strip of grass down the middle of the driveway.

Later, when he's finished, I join him on the porch, where he sits on the bench he made and smokes his pipe. I tell him about the wild turkeys I've seen on the knoll. Presently Floyd comes up and nudges U.J.'s leg. This is out of character for Floyd, who is shy of people. U.J. looks at me in surprise, and I shrug. "This is new," I say, looking at Floyd.

U.J. grins. "He's getting more confident," he says, patting Floyd's head, "now that Max is gone."

I breathe in pipe smoke and pine, and a thrush whistles in the woods. I'm on solid ground.

> Like a true benefactress, the secret
> of [Nature's] service is unchangeableness.
> THOREAU
> *A Week on the Concord and Merrimac Rivers*

bears and scorpions in the shower; or, a week in the woods

Monday.

The scorpion in my shower was a black, ugly-looking thing, unlike the Scorpio I married in my teens, who was not ugly-looking but nevertheless had a sting that would surely make you fester. He became a dentist.

I let the hot water run on the scorpion until it slid down the drain, but I was still reluctant to put my feet where it had been.

Bears won't go down the drain, although they will climb into the shower with you. "A bear would climb right over that wall," Mark said when we were discussing how to keep bears from getting into the dog food. I was keeping it in the enclosed outdoor shower, which is open around the top so you can enjoy the pine trees while you're lathering up. "A bear would come right in," Mark said.

The dog food is on the front porch now, which is not an improvement. But at least I can see the bear coming.

The bear at Mark's neighbors' house was getting into the trash can where they kept their dog food. One day the bear decided to take the trash can back to his place with him. Maybe he thought the dog food would keep appearing in the trash can.

The neighbors called Mark, frustrated. "We have a bear," they said. "It's a problem."

"Back up," said Mark. "The *bear's* not the problem."

Mark, being a champion archer, offered his neighbors a rubber-tipped arrow to shoot the bear's behind with. They didn't think that was funny. But maybe I should get one of those. Then when I see a bear coming, I can shoot him from the porch, and the bear will go lumbering back to wherever he came from, rubbing his bottom. No damage done.

Tuesday.

Summer is weepy in Georgia. I go to bed in eighty-percent humidity and wake up in ninety-percent humidity, and when I step into my sandals the leather is damp, and the bath towels and my workout clothes never dry. Today I turned on the air conditioner. But I did not know that a mouse had crawled into the vent and died, and now the cool air blowing through this tiny cabin, with its single tiny room, with all its tiny windows closed against the weepy weather, is rich with the heady fragrance of raw nature. I burn vanilla-scented candles, creating a combination that is nothing like I expected.

Wednesday.

My sudden brushes with the natural world paint all my days, sometimes with pastels, sometimes with oils in primary colors. Today has been a bold abstract in acrylics. The wasps have been out to get me. They're avenging their dead Kansas relations that I murdered when I let the Wasp Lady bomb the House of Steps with insecticide grenades. The Wasp Lady wore Desert Storm fatigues and carried a rocket gun. At least it looked like a rocket gun. "What is *that?*" I said. She just laughed and headed for the attic. Four years later I was still brushing dead wasps off the windowsills.

Now all their Southern cousins are out to get me. Today their first attack was a *blitzkrieg*. I was about to walk down to the outdoor shower when I stopped to watch a long-legged wasp dawdling on the driveway. It looked like a miniature warplane with its yellow-and-black-striped legs and face. Mean-looking. Lethal, even. When I turned my back on it and started down the steps, it ambushed me and zapped my finger.

Remembering that Mark had said plantain would relieve the sting, I ran to some nearby plantain leaves, chewed them up, and mashed the goo on my finger, then pawed through the first-aid kit in the cabin and stuck on a Band-Aid. Good Lord, it hurt.

75

Later on, I was walking down those same steps when another wasp nailed me on my back between my sports bra and my shorts. I ran for the plantain again but this time I couldn't reach the wound well enough to stick the Band-Aid on, so the plantain fell off. If a wasp had a brain, I thought, then this was a damnable strategy, drilling me where I couldn't reach. I found some hornet spray and went looking for the nest, spraying all up under the steps and the porch, under the eaves, everywhere I could think of.

Thursday.

Some people would have considered, before they went down those steps again, that if they hadn't actually *seen* the nest, they might not have *sprayed* the nest, so they'd better take another route to where they were going until they *found* the nest or they'd probably get stung again.

But some people live in a kind of time warp, where what's happening on Thursday has no relation to what happened on Wednesday, where in fact Thursday is such a long way from Wednesday that Wednesday may as well not have come along at all, and so, on Thursday, those people would walk down those steps without a care in the world and get stung two inches above the ankle, where the skin is thin and shiny and pulls tight across the bone.

Friday.

My daily workout has changed since I've come to North-Georgia. I no longer run down miles of flat road, but make a twelve-round forced march around this steep quarter-mile circle of driveway: up from the locked iron gate at the bottom of the hill, circle the knoll, run back down. No matter how fit I'm feeling, coming up the hill makes me breathe with my mouth open. Today I inhaled a mosquito. Then I inhaled something bigger that didn't die but buzzed around in my throat for a while until I felt a wee flutter and I coughed and...silence.

Near sunset I climbed up on the knoll to look for the nest of wild turkeys that had paraded across the driveway in front of me. I had an eye open for snakes, but because I don't see them often, it isn't a keen eye, and so I shouldn't have been surprised when crashing through the laurel after Floyd I nearly stepped on a black rat snake a yard long. Floyd went on ahead—he never saw it—and flopped down in a clearing. When I stopped, my left foot was two paces from the snake's tail.

The snake raised its head and looked around. I stood still and waited. It lay unmoving a while, then climbed into a laurel bush and stretched out along a limb. Its elastic skin pulled taut over its muscles as it moved, making a glittering pattern of gray diamonds visible down its back.

Saturday.

I never thought I'd be wishing for winter at the height of a Georgia summer, for I do dislike the cold. Even so, a January night without katydids and crickets and tree frogs and Floyd chomping his food on the porch would be a welcome break from all this racket.

The katydids start in at sundown, first one and then three and then twenty and then thousands chiming in until they're all singing in great synchronized waves that surge through the woods and envelop the cabin in a tumult of raucous noise, drowning out serenity and cricket, frog, night bird. Now the setting sun has left brilliant pink swaths behind the trees, which makes the red oaks stand out in dark relief against the white sky. But this visual harmony does nothing to resolve the discord in my ears.

I suppose I should be glad all this noise is only katydids. Earlier I was sitting on the futon writing a letter when the woods erupted with machine-gun fire. I stopped writing, alarmed. What on earth? Target practice at the neighbors'? A militia? A crime? Minutes later, from across the valley and low on the mountain, came three evenly spaced explosions, muffled, as though grenades had been thrown in slow sequence down a tunnel. Then I realized. The Army Rangers from the base nearby must be out on night maneuvers in their playground that is the entire national forest, which starts three feet behind the cabin. This afternoon, the sky was a playground for F-series fighter planes that made my ears ring, along with an army helicopter that hung over the treetops, throbbing like a bullfrog. There is no escape from this cacophony: it follows me wherever I go. I find a rustic hideout where I can't hear road noise and get sky noise instead.

Sunday.

I was reading a World War II novel on the screened porch when a noise made me look up and I spied, at the top of a rotted tree that towers above the others, what Eugenia Price called a Lord God bird, trotting up and down the trunk. This Herculean pileated woodpecker had already made an appearance destroying a pine tree on the knoll, where he pecked the base of its trunk to shreds in search of carpenter ants. I rarely see these shy big birds and counted myself lucky to get a glimpse of him.

In the afternoon, I hiked the Appalachian Trail from Gooch Gap through Grassy Gap to the top of Black Mountain. I recognized Grassy Gap because A.H. and I had hiked up there recently. We'd been examining some coyote scat when a Stealth Bomber, materialized over our heads and disappeared with its escort almost before we realized what we'd seen. Later we found an abandoned hornet's nest and a bird's nest, which we brought back with us, and bear droppings, which we did not.

But today at Grassy Gap I saw no Stealth Bomber, only blue phlox and bright orange butterfly weed, ripe blackberries and larkspur blooming late, and a pale brown silk moth with fractals for wings. A sphinx moth larva, like a tiny boxcar with yellow windows, clung upside-down to a limb. The sick-sweet-smelling black cohosh blooming along the trail couldn't ward it off, nor did it whet my appetite for supper.

On past Grassy Gap is a place where the evergreens have disappeared and a stand of tulip trees covers dozens of acres on both sides of the Trail, their broad light-green leaves close-clinging like small flags waving, and ivy winds up their long trunks like green-flowering garland. The woods are park-like here, empty of the darker pines and hardwoods, as though years ago the forest had been leveled and only the tulip trees grew back, leaving this wide glade open to sky and breeze and sunlight. It gives me the sudden impression, upon entering, that it belongs to an earlier time, and I imagine huts in the clearings, and cooking fires in front of the huts, and paths going down the mountain to the springs.

Now at last I've arrived back at my own hut, and dusk has come, and my knees are creaking from the strenuous hike. I hear crickets singing and tree frogs, one loud in the white pine by the screened porch. The sky is palest blue, and the trees have gone dark, silhouettes against the twilight. A deer is huffing down the hill, and the screech owls have surrounded the cabin: three have perched in the trees outside my window. Their eerie calls, like loons, make me think of Edgar Allan Poe and Ambrose Bierce stories, of haunted cabins and madmen and banshees.

But none of this bothers Floyd, who sits like a sentinel on the porch looking out toward the woods. My novel is in the chair on the screened porch, my soup is warming on the hot plate, and my life is suspended in this poised quietness.

A mourning dove has moved in with the family of turkeys and the black rat snake on the knoll. I hear the dove from the front porch, where I sit and comb the mats out of Floyd's coat. The dove sings near dusk, when the colors soften and the wind dies, before the katydids begin.

It is a restful sound, a dove's low cooing; like a still pond, it holds calm. It is a lullaby, an interlude between the end of day and darkness, a song of muted shades and rising moons and half-light. Containing no menace, it is a sound that unwinds the tangle of knots that have knit themselves together inside my chest like a handful of necklaces that have lain too long in a jewelry box. In this single moment, I remind myself, my whole life rests. I make a cup of tea and hold on to the center, finding no danger to face, no damage to repair, no ego to rebuild.

The most radical kind of politics is language as plain truth.

LESLIE MARMON SILKO

trail tree

Local historian Anne Amerson and I were eating peach cobbler at the Smith House, a hundred-year-old hotel just off the square in downtown Dahlonega, when she asked me if I'd found any trail trees yet.

"Any what?"

"The Cherokees used to tie down one side of a forked tree—usually a white oak," she said, "so it pointed the way to important places, like springs or hunting grounds." She shaped a kind of Y with her hands to show me. "They're all over the woods."

"I haven't seen any," I told her, thinking I'd been hunting trail trees all my life but never called them that. "I wish I would see some," I added.

The Cherokees may have been removed to Oklahoma in the 1830s, but they've left their imprint on these mountains. They're so much a part of the local culture that even the whites tell Indian stories to strangers, weaving them into the patterns of ordinary discourse. "Have you been up to War Woman Creek yet?" they ask. "You know the Cherokees had women to fight." Or, "Cherokee hunter saw a frog once big as a mountain. Named the place Frogtown." Most of these roads were Cherokee trails first.

Where the Chattahoochee and Chestatee rivers converge, the Army Corps of Engineers built a dam to make a lake, flooding sacred Indian lands. I wonder whether any of those trail trees point to Oklahoma.

I didn't know that North Georgia was where the first gold rush took place in this country. It wasn't in California, but in what is now Lumpkin County—part of Cherokee County at the time, thousands of acres that in the early 1800s included all the land belonging to the Cherokee people. Then in 1828 a man named Ben Parks kicked over a rock and found gold. A few years later, the Georgia legislature divided Cherokee County into numbered parcels and gave it away in a land lottery to Revolutionary War veterans and their widows. Thus came the white man, banging on Cherokee doors and forcing the people out of their own houses, rounding them up into holding pens like the one in nearby Auraria, then escorting them west and out of sight. A fourth of them died on the way west, from starvation or sickness.

Still, the spirit of the people remains here, multicolored threads in the pale blanket of the culture that displaced them. If someone doesn't tell you a Cherokee story, you hear it in the names of things. Some words are so corrupted they're barely translatable now; others are from even older native cultures than the Cherokee. But the sounds are there. *Dahlonega.* Yellow. *Walasi-yi.* Place of the frog. *Cherokee.* The principal people. *Chestatee.* Fire-light-place.

In South Georgia the names are *Willacoochee. Okefenokee. Suwanee. Osceola.*

In eastern Kansas, *Oskaloosa. Tonganoxie. Osawatomie.*

In Oklahoma, *Tahlequah.*

Leslie Marmon Silko writes that stories create the world. Words form patterns, like constellations or sand paintings, like the rituals that form ceremonies, and they make and unmake, heal and destroy. Like this *Ur-*language before the Tower of Babel caused it to be shattered, the Word was God, and the Word was One, and it brought all things into being.

Not long ago I got the Word about Pop's farm in Lax, Georgia, where I lived for five years in a shack beside a pond. Around 1930, a black man who worked for my great-grandfather stabbed a white girl to death on that farm. That was the story; thus it was so. There was no trial.

The black man fled in a wagon but was chased by a posse. The women locked themselves in their houses. They were afraid, MaRe admitted, not of the posse with their guns, but of the crazy black man who might stop to rape and murder them on his way out of town.

The man hid, but he was soon found. He was taken back to the scene of what was said to be his crime, strung up in a blackgum tree, and burned alive. The whole county turned out to see it. One of my aunts was there, age five at the time. She said it wasn't unusual for children to be present. Afterward, people scavenged for pieces of rope or charred bone or wood to keep as trophies. This story, reported at the time in newspapers from Macon to Chicago, is part of my family, my cultural, my personal history.

In the seventies I worked as an insurance clerk in Minneapolis while my first ex-husband was in dental school. A Xerox representative came to supervise installation of a new copier. We struck up a conversation, and as soon as he heard my accent and learned I was from Georgia, we slipped into that conversation I often fell into with Northerners, probably because I voiced an automatic self-defense. It was a kind of knee-jerk reaction, when a Yankee found out I was from Georgia, for me to assert immediately that I was not a racist.

"I'm from Georgia but I'm not a racist," I probably said, in answer to the Xerox man's question where I was from.

"You couldn't help but be a racist," he insisted. "It's part of your culture. It's in the water."

"Not everybody from the South is a racist," I retorted.

"Then tell me how you would describe me to someone."

"I'd say you were professional and bright."

"But I mean physically. How would you describe me physically?"

"Well," I said, going slowly, sensing a trap but not knowing exactly where it was, "I'd say you were a well-dressed, professional, handsome, young...black man."

He looked at me. "Why black?"

I blinked. "Well...why not? It's an adjective. I'm describing you."

"If I were white," he said, "would you say I was a well-dressed, handsome young white man?"

"Well...no."

"Why not?"

"People would assume it."

"Exactly."

"But I would have to say if you were Hawaiian, too. Or Italian." I wondered why I'd thought of a Hawaiian.

He nodded. "Yes," he said. "Exactly."

I told this story to people for years as though I understood it, but I didn't really understand it at all.

I once heard the poet Van Brock quote another poet's line: "Wherever I go, the South wounds me." The scholar John J. Gross has written that only when we become sensitive to the ways in which we shape our thoughts in language will we become more aware of what the world has been, and is. I grew up singing this song:

> *The poor old slave has gone to rest;*
> *I know that he is free, free, free.*
> *His bones, they lie; disturb them not*

Way down in Tennessee, see, see.

The pee-oor old slee-ve has gee-one to ree-est.
I knee-ow that hee-ay is free, free, free...

The pickety-poor old slickety-slave has...

The pickety-packety-poor old slickety-slackety-slave...

I sang this song, too, which begins lyrical and slow and melodic, but picks up like a jazz tune in the second round:

> *In the evening by the moonlight,*
> *I can hear those darkies singing.*
> *In the evening by the moonlight,*
> *I can hear those banjos ringing.*
> *How the old folks would enjoy it.*
> *They would sit all night and listen*
> *As we sang in the evening by the moonlight.*
>
> *In the evening (la dee da da)*
> *By the moonlight (la dee da da)*
> *I can hear those darkies singing (la dee da da)...*

As children my sister Kelly and I were in the habit of talking Southern black dialect between us. We did it all the time. We thought it was fun, and funny.

Then came a day in the early eighties when we had to drive Clifton Davis, a black actor and singer, from the airport in Albany to a church in nearby Fitzgerald, where he was going to perform. My mother organized arts events all over South Georgia, and on this day she had sent us for Clifton Davis.

I was in my early twenties at the time, home from the Midwest on a hiatus between husbands, and I was driving. Clifton Davis rode in the front seat with me, and Kelly was in the back with our friend Sherri, the arts council representative who accompanied us. Rain was pouring down, and I was afraid we wouldn't make it to Davis's performance on time, and so, loudly, thoughtlessly, in black dialect, I said something about it over my shoulder to Kelly. She shot back a quip. Then I felt a sharp kick in the back of my seat and realized what we had done.

There was a long silence.

Finally, I blurted an apology. I told our guest the truth; it was all I could think to say—that we had spoken without thinking; that we had not intended to insult him but did not expect that to excuse us; that we had never realized the habit was cruel until that instant; that we were profoundly sorry. In my embarrassment, I couldn't stop explaining, which only made things worse.

I don't remember what Clifton Davis said, except that despite the hurt and anger he must have felt, he was a gentleman. He didn't give us absolution (why should he?), refused to say he understood (how could he?), and wanted us, if I may presume to suppose what he wanted, to try on our inbred racism and see how it fit.

Words make and unmake. Stories heal and destroy. "Why can't they get over it?" I remember thinking when I was young. "I didn't create the past. Why should I have to keep paying for it?" But when you're white, middle-class, and have never been spit on or denied a job or had to eat in the kitchen apart from everyone else, never had to remember how your great-grandmother was bought and sold like livestock or felt up or beaten or raped and torn from her children, never had to fear being dragged from your bed in the middle of the night and burned to death while the town looked on and nodded, these are easy questions to ask. They deny history, suggest it doesn't matter any more; then James Byrd, Jr., is dragged in Texas and proves it does. Histories heal and destroy.

Every afternoon, up and down and around this steep quarter-mile of driveway, I do a twelve-round workout. It takes a long time, and it doesn't help that I am nearsighted and often go without my glasses. This means I have no depth perception. The ground below me is a blur, and I can't see the five lateral ditches that allow for run-off, but can only guess where they are by the change of light over the contours. Often I stumble over them, or on pinecones I can't see, my feet coming down a fraction of a second earlier or later than I anticipate because I don't really know where the ground is. I feel, always, a little off balance. I can't see the ring-neck snakes that cross my path. I can't see the fleabane blooming in the spring or the blue heal-all in summer. I can't see bears.

And yet sometimes I refuse to wear my glasses because I don't like the way they slide down my nose when I sweat. I leave them on the porch with my ice water. I choose my comforts at my own risk.

While guiding me through studying for my comps the second time, Beth insisted that I focus on the writing of oppressed Americans. She had taught at Tuskegee in the sixties; she believed in the power of literature to initiate social change. I resisted. I thought literature should entertain and uplift and inspire, not moralize and preach and posture. "If you do this work, you will never be the same," she insisted. I shook my head at her self-righteousness.

But the Tao teaches that the mark of moderation is freedom from your own ideas. I followed Beth's guidance. I got to know Richard Wright's Bigger Thomas. Ralph Ellison's invisible man. Toni Morrison's Sethe, Scott Momaday's Abel, Edith Wharton's Lily Bart. Dozens of others. When I came to know those stories well, I felt less comfortable with my white face, my Southern roots, my self-satisfaction, and realized I had written my life with a damaged pen.

When I was a girl, an old black woman named Bertha worked as my family's maid. She sang spirituals while she ironed our clothes. I hid in the kitchen and listened to her, and she pretended I wasn't there. I took a Christmas present to her one year after I was grown. She lived in a small house without much furniture. The living room was warm and dark and smelled of bacon, and there was a picture of Jesus on the wall. "I sure do thank you," she said when I handed her the gift. "I sure do thank you." I was so ashamed at her gratitude that I didn't know what to say, and even though I loved her, I could never bring myself to go back.

Theodore Roethke has written, "The word outleaps the world, and light is all." Words make and unmake. Stories are charms. The world is divided. I don't know the answers, but life will teach. Language is a beginning. Words will mark the way.

Floyd on his own

Floyd doesn't seem much affected by Max's absence, except he likes getting two dogs' worth of attention now. Mostly he lolls on the porch, and when I go outside he rolls over and sticks his feet in the air until I pat his stomach.

He's taking some time off, I think, from all the hard work Max used to make him do—running around in the woods investigating noises, going over to visit the neighbor dogs, digging caves, chasing squirrels, inspecting the perimeter. Now that he's on his own, Floyd doesn't seem interested in any of that. It's a dog's life he's living now.

Sometimes Floyd sniffs around in Max's pine straw, or when I drive up after being away he runs in circles and casts excited glances toward the knoll, as though Max might dash down to the car the way he used to do. Or Floyd peers into the woods for long stretches of time, wagging his tail. But all in all he seems to be filling in Max's old spaces without much trouble.

What I'm noticing since Max is gone is that I'm noticing Floyd more. His breath, especially. Floyd's breath could blow up something besides a balloon. Floyd's got the breath that made the first person say: "Man! You've got serious *dog breath.*"

Floyd's breath smells the same all the time: like he just ate a skunk. I don't know why that is, because as far as I know except for an occasional squirrel all he eats is that expensive dog food I have to buy from the vet. But maybe he eats skunks when I'm not looking.

Max never ate skunks, but he did like to make them mad. Max got skunks mad all the time. Every time Max saw a skunk, he chased it or barked at it until it sprayed him. Because of Max, I have a recipe for neutralizing skunk odor. Too bad it can't be given internally.

Unlike Max, Floyd is not naturally curious. He does not go out on long-range reconnaissance, and he doesn't need to know what the racket is. Today some men were hanging out around the bottom of the driveway with chainsaws. All morning they talked and laughed and ran the chainsaws, first on one side of the road, then the other. Max would have run down there as soon as he heard them. He would have barked at them and gotten in their way. Not Floyd. He just lay on the porch, panting. I got my binoculars to see what the men were up to, which was hacking up the overgrowth along the right-of-way. I watched the men, and Floyd watched me.

Floyd on his own

I've seen Floyd sit for twenty minutes without a flinch, watching a deer blithely pulling the leaves off a sapling. Now Floyd sits at the top of the porch steps and watches the woods, immobile. When the leaves stir, his ears twitch. Floyd is not, I think, a formidable dog.

I was making a turkey sandwich when I heard Floyd take off barking down the driveway. It sounded like a warning bark, like Max used to make when a strange animal wandered into his territory.

I opened the front door and stood on the porch, to see what I could see. Floyd was barking madly, standing at the edge of the driveway to my right, where the embankment was steep. I started toward him, calling him, thinking he must see a snake, or maybe a fox—when through the foliage I noticed a kind of blackness where the bank leveled off. The blackness wasn't moving, but because of the density of the laurel I couldn't make out a shape: it was just black. Like a black hole. A void.

Then suddenly through an opening in the shrubbery I saw it. It was a bear! A black bear! An *enormous* black bear! It was the biggest—it was the only—*live* black bear I had ever seen. It was fifty times bigger than Floyd. A hundred times. It was standing on all fours, watching Floyd with an expression like surprise, sort of stretching its neck forward, sniffing, while Floyd inched toward it, barking so hard his back feet were coming off the ground in little leaps.

"Leave it alone, Floyd!" I screamed, then turned on my heels and ran for the cabin. *"Floyd, COME!"*

All at once as I reached the porch I caught a whiff of garbage from the can on the screened porch. Idiot me! Here I am, camping out in the woods, bears in every tree, and I'm dangling spoiled pork roast at the entrance to my tent. Good grief.

"Floyd, *COME!*" I was frantically trying to remember bear-resisting strategy (besides shooting a rubber-tipped arrow)—clap two flat rocks together, talk soothingly to the bear, stand still—when to my dismay Floyd flew down the hill *after the bear*, which was at least two hundred times Floyd's size. "*FLOYYYD!*" I screamed.

I ran out to the screened porch, gathered up the stinking garbage, brought it inside, then ran back out and sprayed the garbage can with pine-scented Lysol and closed the lid, but it didn't help much. I sprayed the whole porch—the walls, the floor, my reading chair, the window screens.

Meanwhile Floyd came back. I grabbed him by the collar and dragged him through the front door into the cabin. He went straight out to the screened porch and stood staring into the woods, a kind of half-mad look on his face like a three-year-old on his first trip to the zoo. Again I dragged him inside and closed all the doors and I was thinking it was a good thing this was Floyd and not Max, who would have tried to bite the bear. In which case the bear would have bitten back.

Immediately I called Mark, who was not at home. Probably out stalking bears. "What do you do when you have a bear?" I said into his recorder, my voice trembling with excitement.

A *bear!* I was thinking. I could hardly believe it.

Then I called U.J. He'd been thrilled about the black rat snake I'd almost stepped on. He'd be elated about the black bear. The whole conversation was in exclamations.

"That's wonderful!" he said. "You've got an entire ecosystem up there!"

"Yeah!"

"You're the only one who's ever lived up there before! You're getting to see everything!"

"I am!"

"But you shouldn't keep the garbage on the screened porch! That bear can smell food a long way! He'll come right through the screen to get that garbage! If he thinks there's food in the cabin, he'll come into the cabin!"

I looked at my bag of stinking garbage. "Uh, I'm taking it to the dump *right now!*" I said.

"Don't attract the bear," U.J. said, "but celebrate the fact that you have the bear!"

"Yeah! You know I was working on that piece about bears and scorpions, and then *presto!* There was a bear!"

"You conjured him!"

"I did!"

"If it's okay, I'll bring Helen up there this weekend and you can show us where you saw the bear!"

"Okay! But I'll have to check with Floyd first!" I said. "It's his bear!"

The exasperating crows have been waking me up every morning for weeks, until a dog down the hill took over the job. She got a head start today by howling all the way through last night, the echoes careening around the valley like mountain beasts until they raced up here to the window above my pallet.

This morning, shaky from exhaustion, I walked down the hill to see if I could get the dog to hush. I found her at the neighbors' house, but the neighbors were away. As soon as she saw me, she leaped around like a happy frog and then played with Floyd for a few minutes and then followed me home.

I don't know what this is. Children do it, too—attach themselves to me, that is. I haven't had any children follow me home yet, but my cousin cried when she found out I was a grown-up. Maybe I smell like kids smell. I hope I don't smell like a dog.

But never mind. I ended up with the neighbor's dog for a few days but Floyd needed the company anyway. Fierce as he is, all he's been doing S.B. (Since the Bear) is lie around on the front porch and wait for me to come out for a walk. Now he's gone off with that Wild Thing from down the road, who I'm relieved to say is no longer sending forth banshees to scream at my window all night. No doubt at this very moment Floyd is escorting her around the neighborhood like the prince of a dog he is, whispering bear stories.

at the dump

I had never been to a dump but it seemed like a place out of a Stephen King novel, ordinary-looking but concealing some terrible menace, like an old refrigerator with an open door. Actually I was going to the landfill, but that was the same thing as a dump, I thought. You drove in, paid somebody, and left your smelly garbage in the pile. Later somebody would come and plow it under with a tractor.

On the way to the landfill I saw a sign: "Landfill closed." Right after that another sign gave weekday hours. I shrugged and drove through the gate.

I didn't pull onto the scale like I was supposed to, and I paid my one-dollar fee with a twenty-dollar bill, which made the woman at the window unhappy with me. She gave me back nineteen one-dollar bills and told me to follow the road around to the left, leave my garbage, and go back out the way I'd come. Just the sort of thing I'd expected.

I followed the road around to the left and spied a green building where some orange-clothed prisoners were unloading garbage bags from the bed of a pick-up. That pick-up had been in front of me at the window, and I had yelled to the two men inside and joked with them about Floyd's bear. "Came right up to the house!" I boasted. "Scared the living daylights out of me!" The men chuckled. "They's bad to do that," they said. I found it strange that they were unloading their garbage in the green building when they had this whole big landfill to put it in.

I drove past another sign. "Landfill closed," it said.

But the lady had just taken my dollar.

"This is a Transport Station," said another sign.

Now what did that mean? They needed to get those signs straightened out.

On I drove, following a rutted dirt road across an acre of iron-red clay fields of plowed-under garbage, looking nervously for old refrigerators and a place to leave my spoiled bits of pork roast I had cooked with so much garlic I'd had to burn incense all night just so I could breathe all the way in.

Soon the ruts began to deepen, and the mud to thicken. The road narrowed to a rocky track that looked little traveled. I was puzzled. Where were all the other people dropping off garbage? Surely I wasn't the only one. You'd have thought they'd keep the road in better shape. There was nowhere to turn around without bogging down in the field.

Eventually the track wound around the edge of a bluff and brought me to the top of a long, steep hill. At the bottom was a clearing, then a thick stand of laurel. On my left, the bluff dropped straight down to a creek.

I stopped. The drive down the hill, soaked from a recent rain, looked treacherous. But I was trapped.

Well, at least the clearing at the bottom was wide enough to turn around in. As for getting back up the hill, I had front-wheel drive and an overabundance of confidence.

Still, I was beginning to get the impression I'd missed something.

I shifted into first gear and started down, broke into a skid, and my brakes locked. Frantically I spun the steering wheel right and left as the car veered toward the edge of the bluff. At the last minute, it slid back into the track and rolled to a stop in the middle of the clearing. My heart was pounding. I got out and looked around. Nothing here: only some blackberry vines. Not even a place for my stinking garbage, the fumes from which were trailing me around the clearing like a bad reputation.

Sighing in frustration, I got back in the car and turned around to face that monstrous hill. It looked far more daunting from down here than it had from the top, especially now I knew how soft the dirt was. My stomach clenched. Here goes.

I shifted into first, jammed down the accelerator, and got halfway up before the car slipped out of gear, died, and rolled back down.

Again I tried.

And again.

Half a dozen tries and each time I made it only a foot or two farther. I was ruining my tires and I could smell the clutch burning. I was trying not to panic.

Suddenly a head appeared at the top of the hill, and then a blue uniform, and then a man, grinning, walked down to my car. When he got close, he made a face and backed up a step.

"Spoiled roast," I explained.

He chuckled and shook his head. "You'll draw bears," he said.

"I already did."

He raised his eyebrows at me.

"You must be wondering what I'm doing down here," I said.

"Aw, you're all right. Don't worry about it."

"I feel so stupid."

"Ain't your fault. I got to put a sign up. I've told her she's got to say to stop at the green building, but she—you know."

"Huh," I said. "Ha ha."

"Just you gun the engine and give it all you got. Since this rain I don't know if I can pull you outta here or not."

I tried a few more times, but still I rolled back to the bottom, and I could tell the man was afraid I was going to end up in that creek. "Let me go get some help," he said finally, and he mopped his forehead with a handkerchief and disappeared over the top of the hill.

Meanwhile, I kept trying. It galled me that I'd gotten myself into such a mess, and the thought of having to call in the Rangers to helicopter my car out of there was just too humiliating.

I got out and walked partway up the hill. A short path angled back from the main track on the opposite side of the bluff. If I could get high enough to roll back onto that path, I could probably make it to the top from there.

With renewed determination, after several tries I reached the path. I was about to go for the top when the man returned with a truck and the prisoners. "How're you making it?" he said, grinning.

"Just tell me," I said. "Am I the only fool who's had no more sense than to drive down this damn hill?"

"Oh, no. One little guy last week, I had to pull him out. I got to get a sign up."

"It needs to be a really big one," I said.

103

As fate would have it, that landfill was full. The green building was a transport station, where garbage was loaded onto trucks and driven out of town.

I might have asked the woman at the window why the sign said the landfill was closed. I might have asked her what a transport station was, since I'd had no experience with such things. But not wanting to appear a fool, I made of myself a big one, and carried my stinking garbage long past the place where I could easily have set it down.

dry weather

Georgia is parched like a desert. I noticed when I was walking today that the rhododendrons are dying. Their long leaves are drooping in wilted clusters and curling at the edges, their healthy, waxy green turning to brown. The ferns have yellowed and begun to crimp, and the laurel leaves are fading and falling to the ground. The long grass in the meadow across the road has stiffened and paled. It rattles in the breeze like straw.

A few light showers have passed over since summer came, but nothing to quench this hollow thirst. Mark says trees are dying on his land, and a watering ban is on: wells are going dry. Farmers in the flatlands are applying for government relief.

This is not the Georgia I remember. When I was a child, the sky clouded and poured rain every afternoon, then faired off in time to fry catfish under MaRe's carport for supper. This summer, the clouds don't come. Yahoola Creek is the lowest U.J. has ever seen it, and the outline of these mountains is far too sharp for this time of year, when it should be softened by a steamy haze.

I want to take a hose and water things. I worry that roots can't go deep enough to find water. What will happen to the bears if all the fruit-bearing bushes shrivel and die? I imagine crowds of botanists examining tree rings from a slice of live oak a hundred years from now, exclaiming over the severity of the Southeastern drought at the turn of the twenty-first century.

I have always worried that the world was going to use up all its water, and I gripe at my mother when she comes to visit and leaves on the tap while she brushes her teeth. To thirst, and no water: a dreadful thought. Like a sail on a windless sea, and the destination just over the horizon.

I've known that thirst—the one for water, and the one for something that satisfies a deeper longing. It was a kind of yearning, an obsession that occupied my waking hours but never played itself out, like a woman who washed her hands a hundred times a day but could never get them clean, like a wish on the verge of coming true if I could only have said exactly what it was I wanted. Then I fell in love with a saint and it all came clear for a few years.

When I lived at Pop's cabin in South Georgia, I rented the movie *Becket.* Peter O'Toole played a stellar King Henry, but it was Richard Burton I fell for. Those blue eyes! That flawless diction! "Please, Lord, make me *worthy,*" he prays as Thomas Becket, and although they were words I'd heard before, said before, prayed before, they struck me like a morning bell and suddenly I found myself on my knees, ready to give away everything I owned. "Lord," says Becket-Burton in his rapture, "are you sure you're not lawfing at me? It all seems fahhh too eeezy." His thirst was quenched, but I was going up in a blaze of spiritual fusion.

I didn't spontaneously combust; I just got busy feeding the fire. I watched *Becket* until I knew the script by heart. I read books on metaphysics. I meditated and beat drums, burned incense and sat zazen, sang and buried feathers, suffered through sweat lodges and vision quests, searching for a cure for what I took to be a spiritual sickness. I went around and around like the Spinning Jenny at the fair, always ending up where I started but getting a thrill out of the ride, believing my search was grave and important and that I was meant to *find* something, to *do* something about the longing I felt in the deep core of myself, the wishing, the *desire*. I asked professors and medicine men, relatives and boyfriends. *What is this?* I asked. *How can I fix it?* I thought I should enter a convent, go to seminary, become a priest. I thought I should go to India, find a guru, become a beggar. I thought I should join the Peace Corps and feed starving children in Guatemala. People shook their heads at me, shrank from my intensity. In the end, the wisest person I knew just shrugged. "When I meet God I'm going to ask two questions," he said. "Why cockroaches, and why this God-blessed yearning."

I called up a medicine man on the phone. "When do I start my apprenticeship?" I wanted to know.

"You already have," he said, and hung up in my face.

Just before I moved to these mountains, when the wind was careening over the Kansas plains like a runaway and the sky was gray and contrary, I found a barn swallow's nest in an abandoned farmhouse in the middle of a field of cows. The nest was an architectural masterpiece, about ten inches long, built from wattle in the shape of a cone against a piece of broken wood that hung from a hole in the ceiling. The nest had a bluish rim; the rest was taupe-colored, its surface swirled with tiny patterns as though the mud had been squeezed out with a cake decorator. Inside this shell, which had hardened like cement, was a nest of feathers and plant down, and under the top layer a single egg remained, punctured somehow too early for the embryo to survive. Barn swallows nest in buildings now, but there was a time when they lived more often under rock overhangs near streams, and if you needed to find water, you could follow them there.

Now, at White Pine Cabin, morning has brought rain. Six days have passed since I lamented the dying of the rhododendrons, and today a storm arrived, and the water fell in plump drops that splashed when they hit the ground and made small rivers in the driveway. I walked down to see whether the rain had arrived in time for rescue and found leaves all over the mountain no longer wilted and curled in self-protection, but raised up and waving at heaven like a thousand hands.

the art of people

Wheeling my cart around the grocery store I am struck by how impersonal it has become. Ranks of cans neatly stacked on shelves and all of us doing this solitary dance with the carts, avoiding each other, getting out of each other's way. No eye contact, most of us frowning in concentration, some carrying calculators, some coupons, some children. Making an awful racket going by the frozen foods because of a bumpy brick floor that makes us feel conspicuous so we hurry.

Even checking out has become a solitary occupation. No cashiers, only a bank of electronics where you swipe your own bar codes. That way, if a mistake is made, nobody made it but you.

This is a survival trick of our species, buying our groceries. We make it a commonplace, but in these times, if it weren't for grocery stores most of us would starve. I might be able to grow a few vegetables or catch some fish in the creek down the hill, and I can build a fire if I have matches, but that's about the extent of my primitive skills. So I go to the grocery store and check the items off my list as fast as I can, weaving impatiently through the aisles, scowling at errant children, huffing at the impudent soul who blocks my way, finding the fastest check-out line and rushing off in my car to do something else.

But what I notice is, when I'm forced to slow down and speak to someone, she becomes real. Suddenly she isn't a transparency anymore, a cut-out of a young woman wearing Capri pants and an oversized T-shirt with her Keds, but a solid, breathing, thinking, amiable creature who home-schools her children and has a master's in mathematics. She takes on a personality, a history, a family, a life, and I'm tempted to ask her, "So how's your relationship with your mother these days?"

While I was in graduate school, I went on a retreat to the Ozarks with a group of students. I sat in the front seat of the bus where I could see, a habit since first grade because of my nearsightedness, and struck up a conversation with the driver, whose name was Larry.

Larry chain-smoked and wore heavy cologne. He had a black mustache and greasy silvering hair that he brushed back from his forehead like Elvis. When he sat down, his stomach sagged over his belt. He wore his collar open and his long sleeves rolled up to his elbows. He and the truck drivers saluted each other when they passed on the road.

Larry had brought along his own radio, which he tuned to a Golden Oldies station and turned up loud when the bus got going. Sometimes he sang along, tapping his hand on the side of his seat in time to the music. I imagined he had a '65 Mustang in his garage, which he took to the drive-in on weekends.

Larry had brought a term paper with him to finish during his off hours, because he was in night school. He was studying to be a mechanical engineer, he said, but his minor was sociology.

At a Laundromat one Saturday, the owner came in and started a conversation with me. His name was Phil, and I soon learned that he had a fix-it business in the back of his store. He also owned the antique shop next door, which he'd named after his daughter who had been killed in a car wreck in her twenties. Now his son was in the hospital, about to have surgery on the arm he had smashed in a car wreck.

After a few minutes, Phil disappeared behind a door and came back holding two bottles. "What I really want to do is own a restaurant," he said, handing the bottles to me. "See, I make my own barbecue sauce. I've won lots of awards. You take these here and go buy yourself a good T-bone." He gave me detailed instructions about how to sear the steak and bathe it in the sauce so I could taste it at its best.

My dad used to play trumpet with a jazz combo that was popular in the Southeast for years. The combo

111

made a few records. Now my dad is a retired accountant who gets a thrill out of using the internet. "Turn it up as loud as you can!" he shouts at me over the phone when he calls to say that the e-card with the dancing red hearts he has sent me is accompanied by a song. "Fly Me to the Moon," blare my speakers, in a startlingly well-arranged piece of electronic music.

"I play it all day long!" shouts Dad, because he never wears his hearing aid. "I think it's terrific!"

Dad has made a tape of Frank Sinatra songs that he swears tells the entire story of his love life, which he wants me to convert into a musical for my sister to direct.

When Dad found out I was going to ride my bike on the MS-150, a long bike ride to benefit multiple sclerosis research, he called me on the phone. "Honey! I don't know how you're going to do it!" he shouted. "It's too far!"

"I'm tough! I can do it!" I shouted back.

"But how are you going to drive home?!"

"Huh?"

"Your legs'll be so worn down you won't be able to reach the pedals!"

Last night he called and asked me how I felt about accordions.

"Not all that good," I said.

"That's what I thought," he said, and read me two dozen accordion jokes.

My dad's a fanatical hybrid of homespun Baptist and Edgar Cayce enthusiast and now he's trying to decide whether to join the Jews-for-Jesus. He wants to be the first

Gentile rabbi. Considering he was once a Gideon, this would be an interesting move.

In the early seventies, Dad bought the first Japanese compact car in Ocilla, Georgia, pronouncing it the wave of the future. He called the car a Su-BAR-u, and everybody thought he was a nut. My friend Cam says he doesn't know whether Dad should be committed to an institution or allowed to shout from the rooftops. Personally I think my dad's a genius but we probably won't know for sure until after he's gone.

Dad's sister, Aunt Helen, is the most consistent person on that side of the family—although in the sixties I wasn't all that sure about her. I thought it peculiar that she took yoga lessons and that her house didn't have air conditioning and that my cousins had pregnant guppies. But I was a country girl, and so I had to make allowances for the outlandish ways of my city relations. The first time my cousins came to visit me in South Georgia, they were awestruck by cows, which they'd never seen before. In a field, that is. In bunches.

My cousins had the first neon tetras I'd ever seen, and the first hamsters and the first mice in cages, which my cousin John Jr. was raising to feed his pet rat snake. My cousins made up words and had a cat and wrote their own music and went to Africa with family friends and caught salamanders and had a neighbor with a horse, off which I fell. They taught me about poison ivy in the woods behind their house; and skateboards, off which I also fell; and banjos, which they could pick and sing to with a wonderful harmony. Now my cousins are lawyers and software designers and entrepreneurs, and they live in Atlanta and Albuquerque and California in varying stages of enlightened self-development.

A.H. is close to seventy but she looks nowhere near it and she has the energy of a twenty-year-old. Small and muscular, she has a dancer's legs and the curiosity of a child. She keeps her gray hair short and soft, like she wore it in college, and her face is open and her eyes are hazel. Her voice is low music. She wrinkles her nose when she laughs. She loves the water.

A.H. rescues native plants from the backhoes of building contractors and puts them in her garden. She can name every plant and knows where she got it and what it looks like when it blooms and what it looks like in winter. She goes off with U.J. to the coast on bird-counting expeditions. She sings alto in a chorale. She grew up a city girl, but she's always belonged to the country.

A friend of mine nursed her adult son through AIDS for two years until he died. After that, she became a Hospice volunteer. She believes in angels and wants to learn more about the world's religions. She often dreams, she has confided to me, of being naked in a crowd of people.

A Thai computer genius designs bicycle helmets on the side.

A Jewish linguist works for the Japanese embassy and teaches sign language and writes stories.

An athlete from Virginia has a doctorate in chemistry.

An ornithologist from New England has a company that designs games and another company that helps rescue the environment.

An award-winning poet from California is a volunteer firefighter, a kendo master, a university professor, a father, and a husband.

Thomas Merton has written that the only justification for a life of deliberate solitude is the conviction that it will help you to love not only God but also people. People are like shades of color in a Monet print I'd carried around with me so long I had forgotten about it, until I packed to come back to Georgia and rediscovered the patterns in it. Taken individually, each of us makes a statement. Woven into community, we become a work of art.

hot chow chow

Along an S-curve on a mountain north of Dahlonega, a
cardboard sign tacked to a tree advertises P-NUT RIDGE. A
few yards farther on, a large man in overalls sits on the tail-
gate of an old pickup in a clearing beside the road.

John Grizzle builds "chesterdrawers" and other furniture to sell, which he keeps promising to bring to P-NUT
RIDGE for me to see. He also sells his wife's peanut brittle
and peanut butter fudge, along with jars of her canned
goods, which he ranks in neat columns along a plank shelf.

The day I met John Grizzle I did not stop for Miss
Minnie's cooking; I stopped for boiled peanuts. Boiled
peanuts were the manna of my childhood and are the curse
of my adult diet. When I was growing up, the Lions Club
sold them at our high school football games, a brown paper
bag full for a quarter. Now I can buy them all year long on

any road in rural North Georgia, fresh and hot and dripping
brine, smelling of late October and harvest nights.

But that day John Grizzle had no boiled peanuts. "I've
about decided I ain't too good at boiled peanuts," he said,
shaking his head. "I shouldn't have put that sign up."

"Is the peanut man coming?" I asked. John Grizzle's
friend boiled the peanuts.

"He don't come when the weather's bad," remarked
John Grizzle, squinting at the heavy gray sky.

Boiled peanuts were all I really wanted, but my inbred
Southern courtesy made me shy about just turning around
and driving off. I walked over and picked up a few of the
jars. The apple jelly was pink and clear as water. Beside it
were grape jelly, apple butter, peach butter, peppers,
pickles, hot sauce, Dixie chow, and something yellow and
peppery called chow chow.

"What is Dixie chow?" I asked, thinking that since I had
come back home to Dixie this was something I should
know.

"Hit's jest a common relish," said John Grizzle. "Hit's
made with cabbage and whatever vegetables. My wife uses
cauliflower. Hit's real good."

"Well, what is plain old chow chow, then?"

"Hit's another relish. That's the most popular. 'At's
ever'body's favorite around here." He raised an eyebrow at
me as if this had been everybody's favorite maybe even
since before the War.

Suddenly I was conscious of my Kansas license plate,
which I'd not yet taken the time to change, and the twang
I'd absorbed after nineteen years in the Midwest that must

have been shouting YANKEE like a cheerleader. "Well, I'll swanee," I drawled. "Whatever do you serve it with?"

"Oh, you know. Jest anything. Vegetables. Meat. This here is the hot chow chow," John Grizzle said, pointing to the bits of red pepper in a light-colored relish. He chuckled. "Hit'll sure perk up a wiener."

I bought enough jars of Miss Minnie's condiments to give my flatlander relations a hot taste of mountain life the next time I went to home. John Grizzle said he'd be back at P-NUT RIDGE every weekend the weather was nice and he'd tell the peanut man he was wanted. I drove straight to town, got my Georgia license plate, and put it on my car. Later, back at White Pine Cabin, I had hot chow chow for supper with my cornbread and collards, feeling like a native.

A man does not know whose hands will
stroke from him the last bubbles of his life. That alone
should make him kinder to strangers.

DR. RICHARD SELZER
Mortal Lessons

succor

On New Year's Eve I went to a mountain party to which only women were invited. Each had written down some quality of her personality or way of thinking that she wanted to give up, so she could burn it in the fire and purge herself. Some wrote complicated letters. Some wrote a poem. Some wrote only a word or two: *Intolerance. Hatred. Judgment. Resistance.*

Around the fireplace at midnight, the women told of work they wanted to do in coming years. Largely they wanted to help with huge projects like ending war or starvation, defusing racial tensions, enhancing education, raising environmental awareness. They wanted to strengthen their marriages or partnerships, their neighborhoods, their communities. They wanted to love the broader world.

This outward-focused generosity caught me off guard; I don't know why. They were women, after all, born with an instinct to nurture, to take care, whether their children were of their bodies or their hearts or their intellects. Most were mothers; many were professionals: doctors, professors, artists, social workers. I suppose I expected more personal concerns: I need money to get my kids through college. I want a new boat. My son is an alcoholic. My mother has cancer.

Spontaneous generosity always takes me by surprise. I'd carried a load of debt with me to graduate school, so when I went for an appointment with a new doctor I was worried because I needed to pay the bill in parts. For fifteen minutes I lay shivering in the air-conditioned examining room, naked as a jaybird under the sheet, so consumed with anxiety that as soon as Dr. Wiley entered the room I blurted out my situation and then burst into tears. He raised his eyebrows, then chuckled and handed me a box of Kleenex.

"Good grief," I said after I regained my composure. "Now you can see why I need that Prozac."

"Yes," he said, and then he took my hand and patted it and looked me in the eye. "Set your fears to rest, dear heart," he said. "Tell the nurse I said to charge you only for the lab work. It's twenty-six dollars. Can you afford that?"

I blinked. "But I want to pay for your time. I just need—"

He smiled and waved his hand. "I have enough money already."

I cried and cried.

succor

"Amy, Amy," he said, shaking his head. "Has it been that long since anyone has been nice to you?"

Trapped! Far more romantic than feminist, the modern woman in me winces when I'm forced to admit it. Yet to quote my old boyfriend George, there I was, "standing in the truth of my life," sobbing with relief over yet another instance of the unexpected generosity that has followed me for as long as I can remember.

And where is the harm, I argue to my independent self, in letting myself be cared for when I need it? I think I lose no part of myself in being loved.

Becoming acquainted with a professor at school, I noticed two small Zen paintings on the wall above his desk. They were not framed and had yellowed from age. In one, a figure was walking over a bridge suspended between two cliffs. He was bent under the weight of a large bag, which he carried over his shoulder. Beneath him was only the vastness of space, and the bridge was narrow and difficult. "That's really how it is, isn't it," I said, chuckling at the painting. The other picture, the barest suggestion of a distant mountain, was equally arresting.

"You like those?" he said.

"I love them. They're so true."

He took down the pictures and handed them to me.

"They're lovely," I said again, and handed them back.

He refused them. "They're yours."

"But Jerry. You hardly know me," I said awkwardly. "You can't just give me these."

"Why not? Listen. A colleague brought those to me from Japan twenty years ago, but even after all this time I've never been able to appreciate them."

"But they're exquisite. I can't just take them. It's too much to give." I put the pictures on the desk and slid them toward him.

"No." He pushed them back. "They're yours. I'm a firm believer in things belonging to people who can appreciate them."

My friend Carol once told me that when she read my books she was always amazed at how much I was loved and yet I never seemed to see it.

"What do you mean?" I said, hoarse with embarrassment. We were in the middle of a live radio interview in Kansas City. "Who loves me?"

"Everybody," she said. "Everything. The world. Your life. The people around you. Sometimes I just want to shake you. Don't you get it?"

There is no remedy for love but to love more.

THOREAU, The Journals

love and kudzu

On a high kudzu-covered hill near Dahlonega, a four-story wizard calls down thunderbolts from the sky. Near the Wal-Mart, a woman holds her hunched grandmother in her arms. An elephant lumbers toward the mountains not far from the cabin, and my friend Pat says she's seen Druids huddling all over Georgia.

It's a natural phenomenon, this Asian vine called kudzu, transfiguring everything it touches. It eats telephone poles, engulfs trees, and smothers barns, turning them into flailing warlocks, lumbering elephants, huddling Druids. When I was growing up, people told me to keep my windows closed at night, else the kudzu would creep in and transfigure *me*.

But you can transform kudzu, too. A woman I met at an art fair pounds it into paper, spins it into cloth, weaves it into baskets. She cooks it and eats it. At a dinner theater, I stared over the balcony at the murder victim sprawled on the marble floor below, a trailing vine coiled around his throat. You can probably even smoke it, although I don't know anyone who's tried. It's only a matter of time, people say, before it takes over the world.

I've been out on the screened porch with the dogs, watching the white full moon, watching the silver shadows move in the woods. There in the dark, in the chill, shivering in my old blue long johns covered with dog hair from Floyd leaning against my legs, I look back into the soft light of this room where a single candle burns and the air is scented and warm. A spirit of romance haunts the air around me now, a remembered comfort left over from past loves and favorite songs danced to at late-night summer parties, where nothing exists but you and that old love and the scent of jasmine, and the whole world is confined to the narrow cone of space you're dancing in. But those nights pass and the old loves leave and new loves come and go and one day it seems you're on your own for good and it's at least half your fault, and sometimes more, and you're not all that happy about it at first but that's how it is so you get used to it, and you stop believing.

So he surprises you, that lion-hearted fellow with the sad eyes who's going to cherish you. You don't see how it's possible, how you could be cherished, you've made so many mistakes, and you aren't sure he's real. There was someone in your past once, someone you let go of when you were too young to know better. He was the one who opened your car door and held your coat and was polite and warm and charming and wanted to take care of you.

He was real, but your friends couldn't believe him. "He treats you like royalty," they'd say, shaking their heads because you were so lucky—and you'd go around wearing his jacket and letting him call you every night, and you knew that he was absolutely *not* two-timing you, and you acted like the queen he thought you were, until you dumped him without ceremony the day you got tired of him, or the day you came back from vacation, or the day you met someone else who was cuter or smarter or funnier or maybe just new. But the new one does not treat you like royalty. Nor does the one after that. But neither do you treat them like kings.

Because you've gotten older and tougher and soon the idea of any other love like the one who treated you like a princess disappears into some old dream, and you think it was just because you were young, anyway, that there aren't really any men like that, not really. At least you've never met one; or if you have, you were a cynic by then and you wouldn't have recognized him anyway. So you go through a lot of years like that, not believing, and it becomes a self-fulfilling prophecy and it always comes true.

Then one day you take a look in the mirror and you're older yet, you're looking a lot like your mother, and there are creases around your mouth and across your forehead. You've had a rough time of it off and on, but no rougher than anyone else. It might have made you bitter, but you've gotten over that. It's winter and the wind is blowing hard, and when you go outside the wind peppers your face with

127

sleet and it's snowing hard, but that doesn't matter, you've softened some, and you're remembering those jasmine-scented nights from your childhood and almost wondering whether there is someone out there, someone who will cherish you, but you haven't got a clue how to find him—and then you drive to town for groceries or a box of pushpins and he steps out of a crowd of friends gathered there in the snow, talking and laughing, and shakes your hand and smiles, and the next thing you know you're taking off your gloves and your green plaid scarf someone brought you from Scotland and you're sitting down to coffee with him, and he's asking you to talk to him. "Talk to me," he says. So you talk.

Then suddenly you take a breath and back up a step. Because even though you think he might be okay he is so *scary*, this man who asks you to talk to him, who is talking to you, who is going down deep inside himself to find his secrets and offer them up to you, let you examine them at the table there while you drink your coffee, in his complete and innocent trust that this will not damage him somehow, and this worries you because you think—well, you know your history.

But then you remember it's been a while and maybe you're different now, and you think maybe it's time to climb over that wall you've built, so you go up and let yourself down the other side and feel around in that dark. You grab the hand he's offering. There is something between you, something strong.

But let's say it turns out he lives halfway across the continent, or he has seven children and a wife in Calcutta, or he's a monk or a spy or something like that. Never mind. It doesn't matter. You laugh, and you decide you'd rather be happy he's been there than sad he has to go. The main thing is that your faith is restored and you can go back home now, knowing it was only your doubt that was blinding you, binding you, knowing there is another who will love you and you'll run into him sometime, and he won't have a girlfriend or a boyfriend or a job on Mars and he won't be the Pope.

So when you feel there's no center in your life, you can hold on to the love. It's all around, comes in different shapes and sizes—friends, lovers, trees, dogs, bears. You take it where you find it and don't question it; life is too short to ask so many questions of love: "Why you, why me, why us, why now, why here?" You put that love to sleep beside you at night and wake up with it in the morning, have breakfast with it on the porch, shake its hand and say thanks for showing up when I needed you, even though I'd stopped believing.

And you're so glad for it, this love that has come back to you, that is in you, and you learn to let it lead you when you don't know the steps, which is most of the time. Maybe, like kudzu, it's only lying dormant while you wonder how it can possibly have disappeared, there seemed so much of it once, when it was warm and summer, and yet all the time it was still there, and it breaks out again like arbutus in the early spring and covers up the world—you can't stop it—charming whatever it touches, turning it into huddling Druids or flailing wizards or circus caravans.

So you can keep this truth in your mind: that wherever you go, and whatever you're up to, there are two things that never die no matter what you believe, and no matter what the weather: there is all this kudzu down here in Georgia, and there is love.

"What if we're in a dream all the time? How do we know this isn't a dream...and when we dream it's not the real world?"
Phelan McKinney, age 5, to his father

the dream

What I know of North Georgia is scents, of creek water and damp moss, pine trees and deadfall. Earth. Mold. Clay. On hot days, I walk by a patch of galax and marvel at how it smells like a skunk. I crush leaves in my hand and breathe in ginger and vanilla; scratch black birch and inhale wintergreen. Walking down a road, I bury my face in magnolia and wild cherry; climbing fences, I'm up to the waist in honeysuckle. The fragrance of these mountains seeps out of the ground and the trees and shimmers in the air, and when you stroll through it, it lights on your skin and reminds you how alive you are.

When I was eight I rode to Clayton on the train from Atlanta, playing my red ukulele to keep myself company. A bus picked me up and took me to Camp Dixie for Girls. It was my first experience with Yankees, which at the time was just a word I'd heard that stood for such mysteries as snow, New York, "Up North," and other weirdness.

Most of my cabinmates were from "Up North," which to a flatlander like me meant anyplace north of Macon, Georgia. They were strange and exotic creatures, these girls, with their finely articulated *rrr*s and *ieee*s and expressions like "you guys" and "wanna come with?"

With what? I wondered.

"You guys wanna pop?" they'd say.

What on earth did that mean?

They had peculiar names, too. There was Dodi, a fairy-like child with dark braids whose hands moved so fast when we played the card game Spit that I couldn't even see them move. And Margo, a flaxen-haired rail of a girl whose soul was black with childhood meanness, who shocked my ingrained South-Georgia courteousness with her unapologetic rudeness. And Jody, quiet, boyish, with glasses, already an expert horsewoman who went on trail rides at daybreak.

These sophisticated children awed me with their self-confidence and fine vocabularies. They were more like miniature adults than eight-year-olds, the opposite of naïve me, who could pick out a tune on a red uke but had never imagined a wider world so different from her polite, quilted Southern town.

I wanted to be one of *them*, savvy and smart, so I started saying "you guys" and "that's gross!" and a month later when Mama came to get me she refused to forgive the Northern accent I'd absorbed, fearing I'd gone over to the other side. "Stop talking like that! That's not the way you talk!" she said.

But those girls didn't have a smell (which was what some of my friends had told me), only made odd sounds like those *rrr*s I adopted for a while. Most everything else at Camp Dixie had a smell. I cut my finger on a broken jar in the lapidary shop, which smelled of burnt rocks. The counselor took me up the hill to the infirmary, which smelled of medicine. The nurse stuck my hand in a bowl of ice water, which turned pink and smelled of blood. "You need two stitches," she announced.

"What's a stitch?"

"It's when the doctor sews your skin back together. He should sew this flap down."

"With a needle and thread?" I asked, horrified.

"It doesn't hurt."

"I don't want to."

"It will take twice as long to heal."

"I don't care."

"You'll have a scar."

"I don't care."

"It's your finger," said the nurse, her mouth a tight line of disapproval.

Camp Dixie had a room full of floor looms and the room was always cool and smelled of pine straw and yarn, and I wove pine straw place mats to give MaRe for a present, and the loom was so large that I had to stand up to use it. MaRe kept my place mats with the ones Mama had made when she went to Camp Dixie in the 1940s.

At Dixie I also learned to square dance, shoot a bow and a rifle, and right an overturned canoe in water too deep to stand up in and so cold you could forget to breathe. The water smelled like ice, which it nearly was. The rifle range, a wooden shelter across the creek from paper targets tacked across a plank, smelled like gunpowder. Square dancing smelled like clean boys, who came over from Camp Dixie for Boys on Saturday nights, and archery smelled like the meadow and bales of straw covered with bull's-eyes.

The stables at Dixie smelled like leather and hay and...well. The riding ring was a long hike from camp, down the road over the creek. I was always early to the stables because riding was my favorite activity, so when I arrived the Intermediate class was usually cantering, which made me seethe with envy. We Advanced Beginners rarely got to canter. We were always trotting, which could scare you half to death, bouncing up and down like a basketball with your fanny not in the saddle and your feet not in the stirrups and your thighs not yet long enough or strong enough to hold you on the broad backs of those well-kept horses. The day after your first ride of the summer you understood pretty much everything about bowlegged cowboys.

At the stables I soaked up all the mingled smells and I always looked to see whether the horse I liked was saddled—the gentle palomino named Goldie, not the stubborn sorrel named Buck who was always laying back his ears like he was getting ready to throw you, which he was.

I wanted to stay at the stables all day. When I grow up (I thought), I will be a stable hand, and I will canter all the time and I will never trot except by accident and I will never let anyone put me with the Advanced Beginners.

On the way back to camp from riding, I was so happy I'd sing camp songs. I particularly liked "Pine Trees," which went to the tune of "Blest Be the Tie that Binds" (although the lyrics could be tricky):

> *Pine tree-ees, pine tree-ees, pine trees.*
> *Pine tree-ees, pine tree-ees, pine trees.*
> *Pine tree-ees, pine tree-ees,*
> *Pine tree-ees, pine tree-ees,*
> *Pine tree-ees, pine tree-ees, pine trees.*

At Dixie, every cabin had a secret shrine where they spent Sunday afternoons in quiet and contemplation. Ours was a place deep in the woods, where the creek formed a shallow pool under the hemlocks. Some took Bibles there. Some wrote poems. One built a child-sized dam across the water and looked for flecks of gold in the sand.

Camp Gay Valley in North Carolina was where I didn't get to play Dorothy in the *Wizard of Oz*. A waif named Megan with long blonde hair and no vibrato got to be Dorothy. I got to be a Munchkin. I represented the Lollipop Guild, the Lollipop Guild, the Lollipop Guild, and welcomed Dorothy to Munchkin Land. At least I didn't have to be a flying monkey.

I was chunky by then and wore black-rimmed rectangular glasses and braces, already a ravishing catch for any boy. Gay Valley was co-ed, and I was in love with an olive-skinned imp named Bunny who was unbeatable at tetherball. I used to spy on him at the tetherball court, where one swipe of Bunny's strong hand could wrap that white ball around the pole at light-speed, which was how fast my heart would beat when I was around him.

One day some of the counselors challenged the campers who wanted to learn self-discipline in twenty-four hours. We would fast, except for water, and keep silent from one breakfast to the next.

At first those of us who tried it were excited and eager, and we wrote letters and read and hiked and played cards and sat by the lake, not-giggling, mostly, and not-talking.

Then lunchtime passed, and blood sugar dropped. Some of us became cross. The afternoon crept by.

In the evening, we hauled our sleeping bags and books and decks of cards to the lodge, where we would spend the night. Now some of us were thoroughly bored. Some whispered. Some ate secret bananas. Some scowled.

I didn't whisper and I didn't eat a secret banana and I don't think I scowled, but next morning before breakfast I went outside and sat on a bench and talked out loud on purpose. I don't know why. Maybe I was like my dog Max, who never could abide fences. Anyway I'd never earned A's in conduct. "Amy talks too much," my teachers wrote on my report cards. "Talks out in class."

So I learned about self-discipline early, but my practice was imperfect.

A thrush sings for hours here in the late afternoon, its melodic whistle piercing the woods like a spear. In the evening, its song is transposed into lower keys by the great horned owl near the spring, the screech owls outside the cabin window, the lone whippoorwill in the meadow at the bottom of the hill. At nightfall, the katydids add percussion, their song like great rattles that diverge and circle the woods and come together again, diverge and circle and return, and I in my reading chair on the screened porch am the center of their joining.

Thirty years ago, around this time of evening, the girls at Camp Chattooga near Tallulah Falls attended vespers by the lake, and we sat on the banks and sang camp songs into the night. I was musical, and even at that age I was always surprised that the most exquisite harmonies could arise out of all that raw girlhood.

Our last night in camp, we carried candles down to the water in Dairy Queen cups, made wishes on them, and set them adrift, watching to make sure they reached the other side so our wishes would come true. Two hundred candles floating on a clear mountain lake at twilight, bearing two hundred urgent dreams, the evening cool against our skin, the fragrance of pine and earth and water on our breath, and two hundred girls' voices, precise and consonant, rising into the sky. We were faith. We were a signal fire. We were a dream as real as any dream.

I never knew whether my candles made it over the lakes I set them out on: I lost sight of them when they got mixed up in the light of all those others. Never mind. For now, I'm content to stay on in my solitary outpost for a while, where the living keeps close by those early days of possibility, and the camp songs are still sung at sundown, and disappointment doesn't last the ride to the far shore.

As the garden suggests a mountain trail, the tea hut suggests a simple mountain hermitage. Everyday materials, unpainted wooden posts and lintels, wattle walls, and thatched or bark roofs allow the structure to blend unobtrusively into the surroundings.

SEN RIKYU
Tea Life, Tea Mind

the way of grace

August has arrived without its usual sweltering heat. The nights are cool, and I've turned off the air conditioner and opened the cabin to the outdoors again. If it weren't for these rough walls, I'd be sitting outside in the pine straw.

In the valley, all the colors have gone to late-summer shades: the lavender-blue of the heal-alls, the deep yellow-gold of the goldenrod and wild sunflowers, the pale silvers and greens of the long grasses in the meadow. The tops of the tall Joe-Pye weed have burst into feathery balls of grayed pink, and the Queen-Anne's lace bows and nods around it in delicate white clusters. A dry wind was sweeping through the mountains this afternoon, whisking away the haze and leaving the air clear. It rustled the leaves in the oaks and sourwoods and made the pines sway. Now a hush has settled in. Floyd is in his dugout under the cabin. Today I have seen no sign of bears.

During the years I lived in Kansas, I visited a sanctuary from time to time, a place where I could leave my busy life behind and hang out in a woodsy hermitage for a few days, where I could move on a solitary, slower track. It was always a struggle to stop marching. I resisted letting go of the part of myself that scheduled, organized, fretted, hurried, and got things done. By the time I could let myself relax into those less anxious days, it was time to leave.

I tried to carry the sense of the place back home with me in my memory: the fragrance of frankincense burning in the chapel, the high tune of the meadowlarks in the brome field, the laughter at meals in the lodge—but its peacefulness always left me eventually. Or rather, I lost it, lacking the ability to say "This can wait" or "You can wait" or, more truthfully, "I can wait."

But from this rustic mountain sanctuary, from this graciously offered refuge, there is no going back. I have been a long time arriving, but I am at last, simply, here. For the present, there is nowhere else to be.

Now the morning haze is lifting, and I've swept the porches and put away the coffeepot. The crows are calling, and the wind is up, stirring my wind chimes and wrapping the scent of pine around me like a silk kimono. Soon I'll take down my walking stick and call Floyd out of his burrow, and we'll join the bears and wild turkeys in the forest, leading our shadows along the mountain paths, searching for treasure, tracking the sun across this blue plane of sky.